CONTENTS

List of Tables   viii

Acknowledgements   xi

1   Introduction   1
   1.1   Background to the project   3
   1.2   The need for research   3
   1.3   Demographic trends   4
   1.4   Community health and social services: poor access and
        low uptake   4
   1.5   High uptake of general practitioner services   6
   1.6   Health experience   7
   1.7   Primary health care in the inner cities   9
   1.8   Aims and outline of the study   9

2   Postal survey of family health service authorities   11
   2.1   Introduction   13
   2.2   Objectives of the survey   15
   2.3   Selection of the sample   16
   2.4   Response rate   17
   2.5   Staff completing the questionnaire   17
   2.6   Identification of the target population   18
   2.7   Perceived problems of access to primary health care   19
   2.8   Priority groups   20
   2.9   Policy and implementation   20
   2.10   Inter-agency liaison and cooperation   21
   2.11   Communication issues   24
   2.12   Service monitoring and review   25
   2.13   Equal opportunities polices and training   26
   2.14   Other service development initiatives   26
   2.15   Attitudes and perceptions   27
   2.16   Future plans: health needs assessment   28
   2.17   Variation in service response by size of target population   30
   2.18   Variation in service response by type of area   31
   2.19   Summary   33

3 Postal survey of general practitioners: selection, response rates and characteristics of the sample 35

3.1 Objectives of the postal survey 37
3.2 Selection of the samples 37
3.3 Response rates 39
3.4 Proportion of black and minority ethnic elderly people on practice lists in samples 1 and 2 41
3.5 Characteristics of sample practices by area 42
3.6 Summary of sample characteristics 47

4 Postal survey of general practitioners: the findings 49

4.1 Recording ethnic origin 51
4.2 Communication and the use of interpreters 52
4.3 Access to female doctors by elderly female patients 61
4.4 Assessment, examination and treatment 62
4.5 Health checks for over-75s 64
4.6 Specific health needs or problems 66
4.7 Liaison with other service providers 67
4.8 Referral to other services 68
4.9 Knowledge of specific services 69
4.10 Attitudes and perceptions 72
4.11 Education and training 77
4.12 Summary of findings 79

5 Interview study of members of primary health care teams: research methods and characteristics of the sample 81

5.1 Aims of the study 83
5.2 Selection of the sample 83
5.3 Research methods 84
5.4 Characteristics of the sample 84

6 Interview study of members of primary health care teams: the findings 87

6.1 Access 89
6.2 Recording ethnic origin 90
6.3 Communication 90
6.4 The role of linkworkers 93
6.5 Assessment, examination, treatment, health promotion, rehabilitation and referral 98
6.6 Over-75s' health checks 102
6.7 Specific health needs 103
6.8 Use of health education resources 104
6.9 Carers 106

Primary Health Care
for
Elderly People
from
Black & Minority
Ethnic Communities

by
Catherina Pharoah

Studies in Ageing
Age Concern Institute of Gerontology, King's College London

London: HMSO

6.10 Attitudes and perceptions   110
6.11 Discussion of racial or cultural issues   112
6.12 Other agencies   114
6.13 Training and education   114
6.14 Summary   115

7 Summary of results and conclusions   117
   7.1 The survey of FHSAs   119
   7.2 The postal survey of GPs and the interviews with
        members of primary health care teams   120
   7.3 Discussion   127
   7.4 Recommendations   131

8 References   133

9 Appendices   139
   A Questions used in FHSA postal survey   141
   B Questions used in GP postal survey   143
   C Questions used in interviews with primary health
      care team members   148

LIST OF TABLES

Table		Page
2a	Groups seen as having particular problems in access to Primary Health Care	20
2b	Service developments for black and minority ethnic (BME) groups, by county and metropolitan FHSAs and by size of elderly black and minority ethnic population	22
2c	Most important ways in which FHSAs can contribute to appropriate service provision	28
2d	Plans for future service development to elderly people from black and minority ethnic groups	29
3a	Type of response, by area	39
3b	Type of response, by sample	40
3c	Numbers of black and minority ethnic over-65s on practice list	41
3d	Number of target patients by sample	42
3e	Approximate proportion of all patients aged 65 and over on practice lists, by area	43
3f	Practices with (i) a Manager, (ii) access to a Practice Nurse	44
3g	Number of general practitioners in practice, by type of area	44
3h	Provision of health promotion clinics, by type of area	44
3i	Ethnic origin of GP respondents, by area	45
3j	Sex of GP respondents, by area	46
3k	Main black or minority ethnic groups seen by GP respondents, by area	46
4a	Whether ethnic origin of patients recorded	51
4b	Frequency of consultation by elderly patients who do not speak English, for white and Asian GP respondents	52
4c	Main methods of dealing with communication issues, by type of area	53
4d	Usual methods of dealing with communication issues, for white UK and Asian respondents	54
4e	Problems with family/friends as interpreters, by type of area	55
4f	Problems with family/friends as interpreter, for white UK and Asian GP respondents	55
4g	Interpreting help received from practice staff	56
4h	Employment of practice staff primarily to work with black or minority ethnic patients	57
4i	Use of interpreters, linkworkers and advocates, by source of funding/employment	58
4j	Action taken by GP respondent on refusal by elderly woman to be examined by male doctor, by type of area	62
4k	Action taken by GP respondent on refusal by elderly woman to be examined by male doctor, for white UK and Asian GP respondents	63

Table		*Page*
4l	Specific problems in over-75s' health checks among elderly black or minority ethnic groups, by type of area	65
4m	GP respondents' explanations for high consultation rates	72
4n	Respondents' views on the most important ways in which GPs can contribute to the provision of appropriate health care services for their elderly black and minority ethnic patients; for white UK and Asian GP respondents	75
4o	Respondents' explanations for low uptake of community health and social care services, for white and Asian GP respondents	76
4p	Topics suggested for further training; those making any suggestion	78
4q	Respondents' views on format for further training	78

ACKNOWLEDGEMENTS

This study was funded by the Department of Health. The guidance of members of the Department in the design and planning of the study in the early stages was very much appreciated.

Several people have contributed to the completion of the project. Janet Askham is particularly to be thanked for her initial interest and help in developing and seeking support for the study, and for continuing guidance and supervision throughout its completion; and both she and Rachel Stuchbury are to be thanked for their extensive contributions to the editing of the report.

Anne Harrop, Christine Barry and Ruth Hancock gave assistance in the use of SPSS to analyse the results. Pat Gay carried out many of the interviews with the health professionals. Sarah Perrin and Claire Whyley helped to prepare and collate the data.

I am also grateful to the members of the advisory group who gave considerable advice and support to the project:

Benjamin Bowling (Home Office)
Michael Boyd (Age Concern England)
Naomi Connelly (National Association of Citizens' Advice Bureau)
Derek Day (National Association of Health Authorities and Trusts)
Dr. Maria-Antonia Manchega (Standing Conference on Ethnic Minority Senior Citizens)
Yvonne Mouncer (National Association of Health Authorities)

Special thanks are due to Derek Day for help in editing the report on the FHSA survey, and to Naomi Connelly for loaning her extensive personal collection of relevant background documentation.

A final word of gratitude is to the researchers carrying out the parallel study to this one, Maryrose Tarpey and Lesley Henshaw, and all other staff and colleagues at ACIOG for the creation of a pleasant and supportive working environment, and for much-appreciated help and encouragement at various stages of the work.

1 INTRODUCTION

1.1 BACKGROUND TO THE PROJECT

In November 1990 the Department of Health funded the Age Concern Institute of Gerontology (ACIOG) to carry out a review of primary health care provision for elderly people from black and minority ethnic communities. The study was to be carried out in parallel with a national survey of social service and health authority provision to this group, which ACIOG was also undertaking (Askham et al, 1995). The overall aim of the study was to describe the health and welfare services available to this group, paying particular attention to the presence or absence of service developments, and the factors associated with them.

This report presents the results of the study of provision within *primary health care* for black and minority ethnic elderly people; the fieldwork for this study was carried out during 1991. The results of the other study are reported separately.

1.2 THE NEED FOR RESEARCH

Several empirical studies carried out in the early 1980s suggested that many health and social services were inaccessible to elderly people from black and minority ethnic groups. This finding, with other factors, has prompted a range of largely local service innovations over the last few years.

In view of recent policy developments, in particular the split between purchaser and provider functions in health and social care, services for this group need to be reviewed. This need has been intensified by the increasing size of the black and minority ethnic elderly population, which is leading to greater demands for certain health and social services.

Future strategy on services for black and minority ethnic elderly people should be based on an assessment of current service trends and the identification of good practice and service gaps. Few of the service initiatives in relation to these groups have been evaluated. Little is known about their success in meeting needs, the lessons to be learned and their implications for long-term strategy development. There is a scarcity of systematic information to guide managers in the future provision of appropriate services.

The scarcity of information and need for guidance is particularly acute in the expanding area of primary health care. The expanding role of general practitioners as both purchasers and providers of health care, the growing participation of primary health care managers in commissioning and resource allocation and the role of primary health care in health promotion make it increasingly important for primary commissioners and providers to be aware of the particular health and service needs of specific groups.

It would be a sad waste if the cumulative experience of those involved in service development were not fed back into future commissioning. It is to these gaps in our knowledge that the current studies addressed themselves.

1.3 DEMOGRAPHIC TRENDS

Both the numbers and the proportion of elderly people from black and minority ethnic groups within the population are rising and will continue to rise for the foreseeable future. The most recent figures, from the 1991 Census, show that while 6% of the black and minority ethnic population of Britain is aged 60 and over, compared with 22% of the white population, 13% is approaching pensionable age (i.e. aged 45–59 years) compared with 17% of the white population (Census, 1991).

According to the 1991 Census, the black and minority ethnic population aged 60 and over numbers almost 175,500. Unfortunately no direct comparison with the 1981 Census is possible in order to examine changes over time. However, it is likely that the number of over-60s at least doubled between 1981 and 1991. It is possible to make comparisons with the Labour Force Survey (LFS) which uses the same classification as the 1991 Census. Combining 1986-88 LFS data, Haskey (1990) estimated the black and minority ethnic population of Britain aged 60 and over at around 129,000. This is considerably lower than the recent Census figure quoted above; however, it should be remembered that it is only an estimate extrapolated from sample data. There are also problems in estimating the total because a sizeable minority of the LFS sample did not state ethnic group.

Within this population the age structure of different ethnic groups varies considerably, and the numbers and proportion of elderly people from black and ethnic minorities is subject to considerable local variation. Some local health and socal service authorities face little change in this population, while some are likely to be dealing with a more than threefold increase since the 1981 Census.

1.4 COMMUNITY HEALTH AND SOCIAL SERVICES: POOR ACCESS AND LOW UPTAKE

Within a context of increasing awareness of the rights of black and minority ethnic communities, a series of empirical studies in the 1980s drew attention to the growing numbers of black and minority ethnic elderly population, to a general neglect of this group by service providers and to low uptake of services such as meals-on-wheels, home helps, day centres and lunch clubs (AFFOR, 1981; Evers et al, 1988; Home Office, 1989).

These studies also noted a lack of knowledge or contact between these clients and community health services. Blakemore (1982) found that despite a high incidence of GP consultations, 99% of Asians and 97% of Afro-Caribbean elderly people had never seen a health visitor, while 99% and 92% respectively had never seen a district nurse. Similar findings on low uptake of social and community health services were reported by all the major empirical studies in this field (AFFOR, 1981; Donaldson, 1986; Boneham, 1989; Home Office, 199; Evers et al, 1988).

Chiu's study (1989) of elderly Chinese people found that one quarter of those who encountered difficulties in bathing and one-fifth of those who had difficulty in dressing received no assistance; three-fifths of those who could not cut their nails and one quarter of those having difficulty with putting on footwear were not assisted.

Boneham's research on a sample of 20 elderly Sikh women attending a day centre in Leamington Spa found half of the whole sample, and all the over-75s, to be suffering from chronic illness.

More recently Evers et al found significant under-representation of people with disabilities from black and minority ethnic communities in district nurse caseloads (1988).

Such evidence as there is suggests that uptake of preventive health services may also be low. McAvoy (1988) showed Asian women in Leicester as making low use of women's services, and Firdous et al (1989) found a lack of knowledge, understanding and use of women's services amongst a sample of younger Asian women. There is little reason to believe that older women, whose linguistic and cultural isolation is likely to be greater, make any more use of women's services. There is some evidence that similar problems occur amongst all immigrant communities, and that the demand for preventive care actually decreases with increasing acculturation (Van Der Stuyft et al, 1989).

The data, then, do not support the hypothesis that low use of community health and social services by black and minority ethnic elderly is due to any lack of need. Most research indicates that, apart from general practitioner services, such clients face enormous difficulties in gaining access to services. Key factors include the insensitivity of service providers to cultural needs and differences, poor client knowledge of English and of the services available, low health expectations, institutional racism, and to low referral rates from general practitioners.

There have been many local innovations, mainly in social care services, aimed at adapting service delivery to meet the needs of black and minority ethnic elderly people. A wide range of different approaches has been taken, which are reviewed in the report of the parallel Age Concern Institute of Gerontology studies. The approaches include the adoption of formal equal opportunities policies within authorities, appointment of ethnic minorities officers and advisers, the provision of completely separate services staffed by members of black and minority ethnic communities, and the adaptation of aspects of specific services to suit different groups such as the provision of translated information, appropriate meals or personal care facilities.

How do primary health care services play their part in the provision of appropriate primary and community services to groups with particular needs? Their role in the delivery of community health services is increasing and is likely to grow further. Secondly, primary health care services are usually the first point of entry into the health and welfare services and provide a key referral point to other services. Finally, and very importantly, use of general practitioner services by elderly people from black and minority ethnic communities is particularly high.

1.5 HIGH UPTAKE OF GENERAL PRACTITIONER SERVICES

By contrast with community health and social services, uptake of general practitioner services by elderly people from black and minority groups has consistently been shown to be good. Various studies have shown high rates of GP registration (Blakemore, 1982; Balarajan et al, 1989); some have also shown a greater frequency of visits to the GP.

Most studies of health service use do not focus specifically on elderly people. Certain trends, however, are likely to apply particularly to older people and provide a basis for reasonable assumptions e.g. those where chronic and serious illness are concerned.

Johnson et al (1983) found that Asian households generally visited the GP more often than others, and that contact rates with the GP were even higher amongst Afro-Caribbean people with a health need, particularly a chronic condition. McCormick et al (1990) in their national study of general practice morbidity showed that men from the Indian subcontinent were generally more likely to consult general practitioners than those of UK origin, particularly for serious illness. Blakemore (1982) showed that while older men of both Asian and Afro-Caribbean origin consulted more frequently than those from the indigenous population, these differences were not statistically significant. Significantly higher overall contact rates arose from Afro-Caribbean women with (self-reported) diabetes and hypertension. Balarajan et al (1989) also found significant differences between ethnic groups in the rate of GP consultation. Afro-Caribbean and Indian men were the highest consulters. Between the ages of 45–64 consultation rates were higher among both sexes compared with white people.

The reasons for high consulting rates have not been systematically explored. It cannot be assumed that high use of a service indicates high consumer – or provider – satisfaction. Frequency of consultation may indicate, not satisfaction with the service, but the opposite. There is some evidence of a lack of agreement between doctor and patient perceptions of health need (Ahmad et al, 1991).

There is also some evidence that the outcome of the consultation may be different for different ethnic groups. In addition to showing that male Asians in their practice had a substantially increased standardised patient consultation ratio, Gillam et al (1989) also showed that native British patients were more likely to leave the surgery with a follow-up appointment, prescription or certificate. Evers et al (1988) found that one of the main factors underlying low use of district nursing services by disabled people from black and minority ethnic communities was low referral rates by GPs.

1.6 HEALTH EXPERIENCE

It is obviously important to consider the extent to which differences in GP consultation rates indicate differences in health status. The findings currently available offer only a rather fragmented picture of the health experience of older people from black and ethnic minorities. The results of the different pieces of research are, however, consistent.

There is no evidence that increased consultation might be due to extra visits for trivial reasons. The data suggest, rather, that members of black and minority ethnic groups are more likely to suffer serious illness. McCormick et al (1990) found that differentials in consultation rates between men from the Indian subcontinent and the UK were greatest for serious illnesses. Women from the Indian subcontinent or the Caribbean were more likely to be consulting the GP because of serious illnesses than were those of UK origin.

The hypothesis gathers weight from higher mortality rates among black and minority groups. Balarajan et al (1989) have shown higher than expected levels of mortality from all causes amongst Afro-Caribbean and Asian men. A particularly disturbing trend is that these groups have shown the lowest rate of decline in mortality from all causes since the '70s, when their mortality rates were similar to those of the indigenous population. While mortality rates amongst the men after the age of 70 drop towards the general level, those of Asian women increase to a level higher than that of women of the indigenous population.

Although much of the work on the health experience of black and minority ethnic populations has focussed on the particular or unique health risks of different immigrant groups, a growing body of research is showing that the major medical conditions and causes of death of black and minority ethnic populations are remarkably similar to those of the indigenous population, with specific health risks in coronary heart disease, diabetes, strokes and hypertension.

Bhopal and Donaldson (1988), for example, have shown that rankings of causes of death, hospitalisation and general practice morbidity in South Asians are very similar to those of the general population. Marmot et al (1984) have shown that the mortality rate from coronary heart disease for Asian men is 19% higher than the UK average, and 28% higher for women. Mather & Keen (1985) in a study of diabetes in Southall found a higher than average prevalence of diabetes amongst Asians of all ages from 25–79, reaching a peak of 13% between the ages of 55–65. Beevers and Cruikshank (1981) showed that there were higher than average hospital admissions due to strokes and hypertension amongst Afro-Caribbeans and Asians; and public health data in Lambeth suggest that high mortality rates for hypertensive disease are due to poor screening and detection amongst its Afro-Caribbean population (West Lambeth Health Authority, 1989).

Little systematic data on the functional problems related to age is available. Blakemore (1982) found that the overall incidence of self-reported health care need for common problems such as in sight, hearing, teeth and feet was similar for all groups except Asians, of whom the highest proportion said they had no problems. A higher proportion of elderly Asians than of Afro-Caribbeans, however, had multiple problems.

The findings described here suggest that there is at least as much need for health care amongst black and minority ethnic groups as among the indigenous population. In certain common diseases health risks are higher for these groups, and may explain higher GP consultation rates. On the whole, however, a picture of minority ethnic health care needs is emerging which is remarkably similar to that of the indigenous population. It seems then that some of the explanation for differences in consultation rates may lie in differential values or attitudes, or in the process or quality of primary health care delivery itself.

1.7 PRIMARY HEALTH CARE IN THE INNER CITIES

To a great extent the quality of primary health care for elderly people from black and ethnic minorities depends on the general quality of primary health care provision in the inner cities. The black and minority ethnic populations are largely concentrated in the inner city areas, particularly in the London Boroughs (Jones, 1991). The Asian population in London is rather more dispersed than the Afro-Caribbean population which clearly inhabits the poorest inner-city areas. The dispersal of Asian communities, however, is confined to a few outer London Boroughs, particularly to certain areas where property values are low.

The delivery of primary health care in inner cities has been the subject of concern for well over a decade. The Acheson Report (1981) identified immediate targets for action to improve services, which included the training of nurses, practice improvement schemes, and the expansion of primary health care teams. Although some progress has been made, much remains to be done (Butler, 1986). Most measures are of potential benefit to black and minority ethnic elderly people. This has been recognised by some Family Health Service Authorities (FHSAs) in their practice improvement pro-grammes. The General Practice Fundholding Scheme introduced in 1990 significantly empowered GPs directly to purchase care for their patients (DOH, 1990, op cit). At the time of this study it was too early to assess any possible impact of the Scheme on the care of black and minority ethnic elderly patients, and so General Practice Fundholders (GPFHs) were not considered separately. Inner-city practices have been slow to take up Fundholding, and although recent extensions to the Scheme have been designed partly to address this, it is unlikely to have had a measurable effect yet on the primary care provided to this patient group. Most of those who took part in this study are practising in the inner cities, and the findings illuminate the continuing problems of primary care in the inner city today.

1.8 AIMS AND OUTLINE OF THE STUDY

Primary health care is the foundation of the health service. As high consul-tation rates indicate, it plays a particularly important role in the health care of black and minority ethnic elderly people. The need for effective, sensitive primary health services has recently been highlighted in the Commission for Racial Equality's 'Code of Practice' (CRE, 1993) which establishes a frame-work for equitable and accessible primary care. In spite of this we still know very little about how it fulfils this role, any specific issues encountered, and how these are approached.

The aim of this study was to show the extent to which, and the ways in which, primary care is addressing the particular needs, preferences and difficulties of elderly people from black and minority ethnic groups, and to explore some of the problems surrounding the development of different forms of service delivery.

The specific objectives were:
- to gather information on any specific forms of provision developed within general practice for elderly people from black and minority ethnic groups, and to review any problems related to separate service provision;
- to gather information on GPs' awareness of specific care facilities for minority ethnic elders and the extent to which they make use of these;
- to gather information on the nature and uses made of any data which GPs (and FHSAs) have on their black and minority ethnic populations in general and their elderly people in particular;
- to assess perceptions amongst GPs of any particular needs of black and minority ethnic elderly patients;
- to assess perceptions among GPs of any particular problems attached to service delivery to elderly people from black and minority ethnic groups.

The study is in three parts:
1 A postal survey of a sample of Family Health Service Authorities (Chapter 2).
2 A postal survey of a sample of general practitioners (Chapters 3 and 4).
3 An interview study of a sample of members of primary health care teams (Chapters 5 and 6).

2 POSTAL SURVEY OF FAMILY HEALTH SERVICE AUTHORITIES

2.1 INTRODUCTION

This study was carried out shortly after the Family Health Service Authority (FHSA) first came into being. It reviews service development at a time when its new relationship with GPs was embryonic. The role of the FHSA since its creation in 1990 has been evolutionary; in 1996 FHSAs will cease to exist as independent authorities, and will be merged with District Health Authorities to form the new Commissioning Agencies, responsible for unified primary, community and acute care purchasing.

While most of this section of the report will refer to the FHSAs as such, it will be the responsibility of the Commissioning Agencies to build on their work, to incorporate the lessons learned into future commissioning, and to ensure that local needs are met through appropriate local health services.

The relationship between the new Agencies and General Practitioners (GPs) will take time to develop. GPs are still independent contractors, and the methods open to influence service provision, beyond ensuring that basic contractual obligations are met, are more indirect than direct.

In addition to a key service monitoring role, the powers available to FHSAs to improve the level and quality of services received by members of black and minority ethnic groups include (a) informing/training/advising service providers (b) guiding/leading through the allocation of discretionary monies (c) collaboration with Health Authorities, community units and other agencies. Commissioning agencies will be able to extend this through joint audit, protocols, needs assessment and contracting.

Those few initiatives which have been documented provide some idea of the general background of service development in relation to black and minority ethnic groups amongst FHSAs. Although they have generally not been targetted specifically at the elderly, this group will have derived benefit from some of them.

The DHSS 'Operational Requirements and Guidelines 1987/88' (1987) drew the attention of FHSAs to the possible obstacles to equal access to health services which ethnic minorities may face as a result of linguistic and cultural differences. It required them to report on specific local arrangements for meeting the health needs of ethnic minorities. The most significant response to this came from Derbyshire FHSA which conducted a wide-ranging review of service provision for black and minority ethnic groups, which it published (1989). This was one of the first attempts to formalise a role for FHSAs in this area of service provision. It identified some clear courses of action which FHSAs could take, and was taken up and promoted by the Department of Health as an example of good practice.

Its principal recommendations were:

- that the FHSA have its own relevant public information and health promotion material translated into relevant languages, and disseminated appropriately;
- that FHSAs explore the possibilities of developing the availability of interpreting services for contractors;
- that practice improvement programmes targetted at poorer inner-city areas (where many of the minority ethnic patients live) be developed;
- that the uptake of screening programmes amongst black and minority ethnic communities be promoted;
- that information on the whole range of family and community health and social care services be widely disseminated amongst black and ethnic minorities.

The 1988 NAHA report 'Action not Words' put a specific emphasis on the key responsibility of FHSAs for the provision, monitoring and evaluation of appropriate services for black and minority ethnic groups. The report incorporated many of the recommendations set out in Derbyshire FHSA's report. It also highlighted the role of FHSAs in the collection of local demographic and morbidity data, service planning and representation related to black and minority ethnic communities. This policy document took a pragmatic approach to service development and offered guidelines, concrete suggestions and practical examples to FHSAs. It received some criticism, however, because these were not based on any systematic evaluation of current initiatives (Conroy & Mohammed, 1989). As already stated, there has generally been little formal evaluation of service developments in relation to black and ethnic minorities.

Only a few of the actions taken as a result of the above initiatives have been documented. It was partly to meet this information gap that this postal survey was carried out. Projects which have been reported include Solihull FHSA's survey of the adequacy of family practitioner services for groups such as ethnic minorities. The survey found that people had little knowledge of the services which were available, or of how to access them. It concluded that much remained to be done, and a great deal more flexibility was needed (1989). Nottinghamshire FHSA reported on its translation of two leaflets on family practitioner services into appropriate languages (Maughan, 1989).

The most important development which has been reported is the increasing employment of linkworkers by FHSAs. The 'linkworker' concept has proved flexible, and linkworkers have been employed by FHSAs to take on a variety of roles within primary health care, including the provision of translation and interpreting services, health promotion and prevention, and outreach health liaison.

Some FHSAs give financial support to the employment of linkworkers or health liaison workers, such as Manchester which contributes substantially to the local Chinese medical centre.

Underlying these schemes is the recognition that while many patients in an area can benefit from such services, it is often economically impracticable for one GP to employ a linkworker. There are potentially many benefits from FHSA employment of linkworkers. One is that GPs may be able to have access to a number of linkworkers, and a wider range of linguistic and cultural expertise. Another is that they can employ linkworker services on a part-time basis. It also means that the linkworkers are independent of the GPs, and may be able to play more of an advocacy role on behalf of their patients where they feel it is necessary. The model also provides scope for linkworkers to be employed to look at complete service areas related to black and ethnic minorities, and not just to meet the day-to-day needs of individual patients and health professionals.

The provisions of the Operational Requirements and Guidelines 1987/88 mean that there is now wider scope for the employment of linkworkers in primary care, and it is important to assess developments and ensure that the most effective use is made of these resources.

The 1990 GP Contract emphasised the need for a close working relationship between GPs and FHSAs. The provision of care for black and ethnic minorities is one area where future partnerships with commissioning agencies will be important.

2.2 OBJECTIVES OF THE SURVEY

It was decided to carry out a small scale study of FHSA initiatives in service provision for elderly people from black and minority ethnic groups, with an emphasis on information which might be relevant to service development at practice level. Comparisons could then be drawn between approaches to this patient group at FHSA level and at practice level.

The objectives of the survey were therefore to assess:
- the extent of service developments in family practitioner care which would benefit black and minority ethnic elderly people;
- the nature of FHSA approaches to service developments for black and minority ethnic people in general, and any general trends or patterns in methods of provision;
- whether the extent of service development for this group was more related to interests in elderly people or in black and minority ethnic communities;

- any priority being given to elderly people from black and minority ethnic communities.

The scope of the study was limited, partly by the budget for the whole project but, more importantly, by the need to avoid placing heavy demands on FHSA staff at a time of considerable pressure. During the survey it became apparent that many FHSA staff were interested in early feedback on the approaches to service development in this area; there was a high level of interest and co-operation with both this survey and the preparatory work for the postal survey of GPs.

2.3 SELECTION OF THE SAMPLE

FHSAs were selected for the study by the size of their elderly black and minority ethnic population. In estimating this population, it was necessary to make some allowance for its significant growth since the 1981 Census, which has produced much higher rates of increase in certain places than in others (the findings of the 1991 Census were not available at the time of the study). The selection of areas was therefore based on the aggregate of black and minority ethnic population of pensionable age or approaching pensionable age (45 years or over) as identified in the 1981 Census.

A cut-off point of 1500 persons of or approaching pensionable age was chosen. Although this cut-off point was arbitrary it provided a representative sample of the main areas where the population born overseas was likely to live. It also allowed for the inclusion of areas which were known to have recent new settlement. In fact, FHSAs selected for the study were responsible for family practitioner services to the vast majority of the black and minority ethnic elderly population in England.

A further factor which had to be taken into account in the selection of FHSAs was the difference between their boundaries and those of the Census enumeration districts. For some FHSA areas, the figures for different Census districts had to be aggregated.

A final total of 55 FHSA areas, 55% of the total number, was included in the sample. Within these areas, of course, the actual distribution of the population varied enormously. While some of the London and other metropolitan FHSAs had very significant black and minority ethnic populations spread throughout much of their area, the population of others was concentrated in one or two known large centres or was more widely and thinly dispersed throughout. It was hoped that the survey would reveal any influence of this variation on service development for this group.

All Regional Health Authorities[1] except Northern were represented. All FHSAs in the Oxford Region were included, and all except two in the four Thames Regions. A majority of the FHSAs in each of the East Anglian, Wessex, South Western and West Midlands Regions were included.

2.4 RESPONSE RATE

A high response rate was obtained: 44 FHSAs (80%) returned completed questionnaires. Analysis of respondents and non-respondents showed that there were some differences between the two groups.

Eight (73%) of the non-respondents covered metropolitan districts, compared with 23 (52%) of the respondents. Five (45%) of the non-respondents were London Borough areas, compared with eleven (25%) of the respondents; four of these five non-respondents covered outer London borough areas (with the exception of one inner London borough included within their boundaries). This means that the outer London borough areas, within which there are some large black and ethnic minority communities, were somewhat under-represented within the survey.

The average proportion of black and minority ethnic elderly people amongst the elderly population as a whole was 1.8% for the non-respondents, compared with 1.3% for the respondents. This result is consistent with the higher proportion of metropolitan districts, where there are some concentrations of black and minority ethnic populations, among the non-respondents.

These differences are not likely to have biased the survey results significantly. As will be shown later in this report, there is little evidence of a strong relationship between service development and either (a) type of area, or (b) numbers and proportion of black and minority ethnic elderly peole in the area.

2.5 STAFF COMPLETING THE QUESTIONNAIRE

There was not thought to be any common title or post for those staff with an interest in or specific remit for services specifically for black and minority ethnic groups. For this reason FHSAs were asked to record the job title of the person who completed the questionnaire. It was not always clear whether differences in title represented differences in function, particularly where staff

---

1 This study was carried out before the re-configuration of the Regional Health Authorities proposed in 1993.

involved in planning were concerned. The categories used may not be totally mutually exclusive. The job titles of those who completed the questionnaire were:

General manager	9
Planning and information manager/officer	23
Planning and operations/development manager	6
Special projects officer	1
Ethnic minorities development officer	2
Medical director	2
Health promotion officer	1

In the findings which follow it should be borne in mind that although the respondents are referred to as the FHSAs themselves, the actual respondents are the individuals as specified above.

2.6 IDENTIFICATION OF THE TARGET POPULATION

2.6.1 Information on population

One of the most significant of the new responsibilities of FHSAs is to assess needs and plan services in their areas. FHSAs were asked whether they had any information on the ethnic composition of the population they served.

In response, 38 (86%) of the FHSAs said that they had information on the ethnic composition of their local populations. Only 28 responded to a request for further details of the type of data kept, and the majority of these referred to the 1981 Census data, or other census derived sources, such as the Jarman indexes (which are used nationally as a measure of deprivation and include a weighting for component of population from black and minority ethnic group). Three said they had entered or were entering data on ethnic origin into their patient databases; two of these were doing it by surname trawl. The level of detail which FHSAs had on the location and ethnic structure of local communities varied considerably. Although only FHSAs with significant black and minority ethnic populations were included within the survey, one denied there were any, while others gave ward breakdowns by specific ethnic group or sub-group, percentage and sometimes even numbers by area or street.

It was clear that in some areas Census-based information had been supplemented by local knowledge or surveys from a variety of sources, including local community groups, academic departments, and local authorities. The majority of FHSAs, however, appeared to have little other than 1981 Census information at present. Four FHSAs had no information at all, and two did not answer the question.

In terms of targetting services, ward level percentages by Census group are anyway a very crude measure, indicating little about the particular age, socio-economic and ethnic structure of specific areas and of the likely character of the lists of particular GPs. If the allocation of development money is to take account of the structure of local or GP based populations, then many FHSAs are far from having the information needed.

Detailed local demographic and morbidity information is particularly important where black and minority ethnic groups are concerned, because of the considerable geographical variation in the age and ethnic structure of these populations. To get a more specific picture, one FHSA had decided to carry out a detailed in-depth survey of need and differential health experience within the population of one ward. This seems a particularly feasible and valuable approach, whose results and method could be usefully disseminated to other FHSAs.

2.6.2 Means of collecting data

FHSAs were also asked whether they had any means of collecting data on the ethnic origins of their patient population. Only 12 (27%) said they had or were developing means of setting up their own databases on ethnic origins: of these, four mentioned surname surveys, three referred to use of the annual practice composition reports, and two referred to working groups on the subject. It is clear that FHSAs still had some way to go in this area.

The collection of data on the ethnic composition of local populations was seen as problematic:

> "Potentially by asking GPs – practice lists vary a great deal from ward/parish composition. This would be very complex and difficult – not just about origins, but ethnicity and colour, self-perception"
>
> "Practice plans could contain this information – we would encourage this. However it is not included in mandatory GP terms of service information that GPs have to provide in annual reports/plans/profiles. Will therefore be a slow process of support and facilitation."

2.7 PERCEIVED PROBLEMS OF ACCESS TO PRIMARY HEALTH CARE

FHSAs were asked in a multiple choice question whether they considered any specific groups in their area to have particular problems in access to primary health care. The results are shown in Table 2a.

These results suggest that FHSAs perceive elderly people in general as experiencing some difficulty in access to primary health care. Black and minority ethnic elderly people may experience additional difficulty, but are seen as sharing the common problems of their age-group.

Table 2a: Groups seen as having particular problems in access to primary health care

	No.	%
Black and ethnic minority elderly	10	23
Over 60/65s in certain parts of FHSA area	9	20
Over 75s	9	20
Elderly people in residential care	4	9
Elderly mentally infirm people	1	2
Travellers	1	2
No particular group	2	5
No information	5	11
Not answered	23	52
Total respondents (base for %)	44	

NB: *Percentages add to more than 100 as some FHSAs gave multiple responses*

2.8 PRIORITY GROUPS

FHSAs were asked if they had prioritised any particular groups of elderly people in terms of resource allocation, service review, etc., and if so, which groups and in what way. Fifteen (34%) said they had, but the majority of these referred to the over-70s.

The provision for over-75s' health checks has obviously been important in giving people aged 75 and over greater prominence. Although the health checks afford an opportunity to make contact with black or minority ethnic elderly people, only two FHSAs reported taking measures to ensure that the over-75s' health checks were equally accessible to all, and that facilities were available for full assessments to be carried out. Measures included monitoring the appropriateness of letters and other ways of publicising checks, and employing specific linkworker staff for health checks amongst elderly people from black and minority ethnic groups.

2.9 POLICY AND IMPLEMENTATION

In addition to the open-ended questions on approaches, developments and priorities, FHSAs were asked a multiple choice question on whether they had undertaken any of a number of specific measures in relation to services for black and minority ethnic groups. These were measures generally aimed at black and minority ethnic communities, from which their elderly people might benefit, but which were not necessarily targeted specifically at this group. The following question asked whether they had undertaken any service development initiatives in relation to black and ethnic minorities, apart from those mentioned in the multiple choice question. They were then asked whether any of the initiatives mentioned in response to either of these questions were targetted specifically at elderly people.

It needs to be stressed that these questions were designed only to elicit systematic information on approaches taken by FHSAs. They were not in any sense intended as performance indicators: too little is known about outcomes for any such assessment to be meaningful. Some of the measures related to the standards of good practice set out in key FHSA policy documents, some were about the roles, responsibilities and discretionary powers set out in the White Paper, and some were related to the implementation of equal opportunities policies in general. Table 2b summarises the results.

2.10 INTER-AGENCY LIAISON AND COOPERATION

General strategies for future health and social service provision are likely to involve increasing partnership between authorities. Inter-agency collaboration has been generally recognised as vital to the development of good services for black and minority ethnic communities.

In response to the multiple choice question reported above, 32 FHSAs (73%) reported that they had sought advice from their DHA in relation to this patient group, while 27 (61%) said they had sought advice from their local authority. Some pointed out that the exchanges had been reciprocal. Unfortunately the questionnaire could not explore these relationships in detail, but several FHSAs described collaborative ventures in response to an open question on other service development initiatives in relation to black and minority ethnic groups. For example, one FHSA pointed out that community care is one area where the need for inter-agency cooperation in relation to black and minority ethnic patients is particularly important:

> *"(we are) working in partnership with the health authorities and local authorities to develop policies for the provision of minority ethnic sensitive and appropriate family health services, particularly through the production of the client specific community care plan."*

Another FHSA was participating in the production of a joint statutory/ voluntary sector information pack for black and minority ethnic groups.

As might be expected, more FHSAs described collaborative initiatives with District Health Authorities than with other agencies. Joint service developments reported included local health promotion action, including the production of appropriate audio-visual material, surveys and service monitoring exercises, and projects such as holding health 'fairs', joint employment of health liaison officers and linkworkers, and targetting local 'health action'

Table 2b: Service developments for black and minority ethnic (BME) groups, by county and metropolitan FHSAs, and by size of elderly black and minority ethnic population

	Total		County	Metropolitan	BME pop. 7% or lower	BME pop. over 7%
	No.	%	No.	No.	No.	No.
FHSA has sought advice/information from DHA	32	73	14	18	15	17
FHSA has sought advice/information from LA	27	61	12	15	13	14
FHSA maintains list of interpreting services	10	23	3	7	5	5
FHSA keeps record of languages spoken by GPs/ practice staff	36	82	17	19	17	19
FHSA employs ethnic minority development officer	7	16	2	5	3	4
FHSA has/used to have working group on ethnic minorities	9	21	2	7	4	5
FHSA consumer survey identifying views of black and minority groups	7	16	2	5	4	3
FHSA review of services to black and minority ethnic groups	12	28	6	6	6	6
FHSA monitoring of service use by black and ethnic minorities	3	7	1	2	–	3
FHSA adoption of equal employment policy	30	68	15	15	15	15
FHSA has had leaflets/posters translated	25	57	11	14	13	12

FHSA has advised GPs on issues of black and ethnic minorities	9	21	3	6	5	4
FHSA has advised other practitioners on such issues	4	9	3	1	1	3
FHSA gives/has given training on equal opportunities	3	7	2	1	2	1
FHSA has funded GP training/education on equal opportunities	1	2	–	1	–	1
Total respondents (base for %)	44	21	23	22	22

neighbourhoods and service priorities. One FHSA said it was hoping to employ someone specifically to develop links with District Health Authorities.

Many of these initiatives were not aimed directly at black and minority ethnic communities, but were seen as comprehensive service review measures, with the scope to target or highlight a range of specific needs, including those of black and minority ethnic groups. The general picture to emerge is that although there are variations in the breadth and depth of inter-agency contact over needs and services for black and minority ethnic patients, some important foundations are being laid.

2.11 COMMUNICATION ISSUES

2.11.1 Translation and interpretation

As many as 36 FHSAs (82%) reported that they kept a record of languages spoken by GPs in their area and 25 (57%) had had posters or leaflets translated.

These results suggest that, consistent with other health authorities and departments, FHSAs have focussed on interpreting and translating facilities in considering service initiatives for members of black and minority ethnic groups. These are services from which elderly people may particularly benefit, since high proportions have limited knowledge of English. There is also evidence, however, that black and minority ethnic patients choose GPs mainly by language (Ahmed et al, 1989). The impact of translation services and translated material of various kinds needs to be evaluated.

2.11.2 Linkworkers and advocates

That the communication problems of black and minority ethnic patients lie as much in differences of class and culture as language has been widely recognised, and has prompted formal provision for the employment of linkworkers in primary health care. FHSAs were asked whether they directly employed any linkworkers: six (14%) said they did. A few others made or had made a contribution to the cost of linkworkers employed by their DHA. They were also asked whether any GPs in their area employed linkworkers: twelve (27%) said that they did.

In Kensington and Chelsea linkworkers were involved in over-75s' health checks. Some linkworkers were regarded as advocates, particularly in City and East London, where the FHSA had developed and implemented a six-month full time training course for bilingual advocates to work in primary health care, in conjunction with the local Department of General Practice and Primary Care.

In view of the high numbers of FHSAs which had implicitly acknowledged language difficulties in their area by maintaining registers of languages spoken by GPs and by translating leaflets etc., the numbers of linkworkers employed appears low. The range of schemes already in existence demonstrates how much can be achieved where FHSAs either make flexible use of their own funds or persuade GPs to group together to fund linkworkers, with the FHSA possibly holding the contract. Many FHSAs, however, still see the employment of linkworkers as primarily a GP responsibility. Several comments implied this:

> *"The FHSA's policy is to encourage GPs to make bids for staff to work with ethnic minorities"*
>
> *". . . by encouraging GPs to develop practice profiles which will then inform their views on the sort of service they should be providing particularly with regard to the employment of practice staff"*
>
> *"The employment of a linkworker has been offered to GPs, but so far, has not been considered an immediate priority by GPs themselves"*
>
> *"We are . . . in the position of being only proxy providers – the GPs do the actual service delivery and we can advise and encourage but not insist".*

The GP postal survey gives some insight into GP attitudes towards the value of employing linkworkers. It is possible that FHSAs may need to take a stronger lead in encouraging GPs or in employing linkworkers themselves.

Only three FHSAs (7%), however, mentioned the employment of linkworkers as part of their future plans.

2.12 SERVICE MONITORING AND REVIEW

Again according to the responses to the multiple choice question on service approaches, seven FHSAs (16%) had carried out a consumer survey amongst black and ethnic minority communities. Twelve (28%) had reviewed services to black and minority ethnic groups, but only three reported monitoring actual service use by them. These particular exercises were not targetted at the elderly, but one FHSA had carried out a survey of access problems amongst the elderly population as a whole.

Although it would have been unrealistic to expect FHSAs to have carried out much monitoring since the implementation of the new Contract, it did appear that service monitoring was only just getting off the ground. Only one FHSA mentioned that it was monitoring the outcome of over-75s' health checks and that this exercise could be used to assess any specific health issues among black and minority ethnic elderly people. Service monitoring was not mentioned in the open questions on the most important ways in which FHSAs can contribute to services for black and minority ethnic elderly, or in any future plans for service development to this group (see Tables 2c and 2d). Clearly there is scope for much more work of this kind, particularly in view of the well-documented access problems of this patient group.

2.13 EQUAL OPPORTUNITIES POLICIES AND TRAINING

Again in response to the multiple choice question, only nine FHSAs (21%) said that they had given advice to GPs on services to black and minority ethnic communities. In general, training initiatives had received little attention: only three FHSAs (7%) said they had funded or provided any equal opportunities training.

FHSAs are well-placed to take a lead in setting standards in equal opportunities for their contractor GPs and practice staff through education and training, and there is scope for them to do much more in this. Sandwell FHSA has investigated the need for further training or education in relation to black and minority ethnic communities, through a small qualitative survey of the attitudes and problems of local GPs.

Thirty FHSAs (68%) said they had an equal opportunities employment policy. Although it has been shown that adoption of formal equal opportunities policies does not bear a direct relationship to implementation of equal opportunities programme, it is now accepted as a matter of fundamental good practice.

2.14 OTHER SERVICE DEVELOPMENT INITIATIVES

Certain FHSAs have been specifically targetting the needs of their local black and minority ethnic communities for some time. Seven (16%) reported employing minority ethnic development officers.

Nine (21%) had participated or were participating in working groups. These, unless they have a very specific brief, are usually an indication that developments are at an early stage, and it was clear from the details given by one FHSA that its working group was the first step in looking at this area of need.

Some FHSAs reported a strategy of targetting certain inner-city practices for practice improvement programmes. Many black and minority ethnic communities live in stressed inner urban areas. The employment of a primary care facilitator is often central to the implementation of this policy, and an important aim is to encourage practitioners to employ practice nurses. The services of practice nurses can be particularly relevant to older people with chronic conditions, and in the over-75s' health checks. Where practice nurses are from black or minority ethnic communities themselves they seem to be particularly important in extending primary care services to local populations, although evidence for this is still mainly anecdotal.

Another area mentioned in response to the open question on service initiatives was health promotion. A few FHSAs said they had included specific responsibilities for health promotion in the job description of their linkworker. Health promotion nurses or facilitators were also employed by a few FHSAs: some had a specific remit for services to black and minority ethnic populations, while others were working within practices with large black and minority ethnic populations and developing clinics aimed at elderly people. These are exciting developments with the potential to benefit patient groups who have hitherto had little contact with community health services. The success of these initiatives in reaching such groups has yet to be assessed. Other initiatives mentioned included a financial contribution towards an Asian magazine programme to provide health promotion advice, and setting up a 'health for all' conference in an area of high minority ethnic residence.

2.15 ATTITUDES AND PERCEPTIONS

To assess more general attitudes, an open question was asked on the most important ways in which FHSAs thought they could contribute to the provision of appropriate primary health care services to black and minority ethnic elderly. Table 2c summarises the responses.

Table 2c: Most important ways in which FHSAs can contribute to appropriate service provision

	No	%
Translation of information	15	34
Training and education	12	27
Improved access	9	20
More liaison with LAs	8	15
Employment of linkworkers	8	18
Receptive/sensitive attitudes	7	16
Improved community liaison	7	16
Improved data/statistics	4	9
More carer support	2	5
No reply	10	23
Total respondents (base for %)	44	

NB: Percentages add to more than 100 because some FHSAs gave more than one response

Ten (23%) of the FHSAs did not answer this question. Amongst those who did there was a wide spread of responses. These consisted mainly of specific measures.

Some FHSAs saw a need for guidelines on particular aspects of practice; issues mentioned included how to determine the most appropriate allocation of linkworker time per practice, standards for interpreters and interpreting services, and training for linkworkers.

The results for this question did not show any priority being given to more strategic approaches, other than the importance attached to health needs assessment which has been discussed earlier. In fact in the survey as a whole only four FHSAs gave any importance to mechanisms to ensure appropriate service provision for black and minority ethnic communities across the board, and, as the following quotations illustrate, these were expressed more as principles than as practical strategies:

> "(There must be) reference to minority ethnic needs within all
> objectives to ensure the issue is taken on board at every level"
> "Ethnic health issues are to be the responsibility of directors and senior
> managers"

Two of these four FHSAs placed the interests of black and minority ethnic patients firmly within the context of quality assurance programmes designed to ensure a high quality of service to all individual patients. The number of non-respondents to this question, and the absence of any consistency in the answers given, suggest either that individual FHSAs do not yet have a clearly defined approach to this area of service development, or that any strategies have not yet been communicated and agreed broadly within the management structures of individual organisations. Without any strategic policy, issues can only be addressed on an ad hoc, piecemeal basis.

2.16 FUTURE PLANS: HEALTH NEEDS ASSESSMENT

FHSAs were asked a further open question on whether they had any plans for future service development to elderly people from black and minority ethnic groups. Only 23 FHSAs (52%) said they did have plans. Table 2d shows their responses.

The plan most often mentioned was a needs survey: many FHSAs were planning to carry out local population or needs surveys, often in collaboration with the other major statutory service providers. Other responses were widely spread and mainly concerned different service development measures which reflected the stage of development of the individual FHSA. There was

Table 2d: Plans for future service development to elderly people from black and minority ethnic groups

	No.	%
Needs survey	13	29
More collaboration with other agencies	5	11
More/better interpreting/translating	5	11
Employment of service advisers	4	9
Employment of linkworkers	3	7
Targetted health promotion	2	5
No reply	21	48
Total respondents (base for %)	44	

NB: Percentages add to more than 100 because some FHSAs gave more than one response

no suggestion that FHSAs were moving towards any consensus on policy, or planning any broad shifts of approach or emphasis in the near future.

In general health needs assessment was frequently mentioned throughout the questionnaires, and seemed to have a high priority. This suggests that many FHSAs still felt unclear about the needs of their local black and minority ethnic communities and how best to target their resources. Some were not convinced that specific needs or problems existed:

> *"(this) FHSA is undertaking a review of outcomes of assessment of over-75s, following new contract. If this reveals problems of equity and access for this group, action plan will be devised".*

The responses revealed different approaches to appropriate ways of carrying out health needs assessment. One FHSA expressed a clear view that priorities have to be determined by the disease patterns of the population as a whole:

> *"while (black and minority ethnic elderly people) are recognised as an important subset of their populations, service developments are based on whole populations."*

The importance of disease-based assessment is echoed in other comments, for example:

> *"(our approach is) primarily through needs assessment work, which will look at differential disease experience of different ethnic groups, and how their needs vary because of this."*

This view assumes that disease-based assessments will reveal the differences in need, but in fact there is little evidence that the major health needs of this group are very different from those of other elderly people. What has been well established by research is that there are significant differences in need related to methods of service delivery.

It is clear that for some FHSAs, however, such local needs surveys appear to be seen as a prerequisite to formulating any priorities or strategies in relation to black and minority ethnic elderly. There are some difficulties with this approach. Firstly, while assessment is being undertaken, needs may go unmet. Secondly, even where local assessment indicates need, the key determinant in resource allocation will be decisions about priorities. Small groups, such as black and minority ethnic elderly, may not attract a high priority. Several FHSAs had taken a more pluralistic approach to needs identification. One claimed that two perspectives are needed:

> *"the Public Health perspective, the incidence of disease; and from Community Groups via consumer affairs departments. (The FHSA) should ensure the development of services with people committed to their cause."*

Another identified a key role for the community development approach in assessing need, stating that a health promotion activity in the community which focussed on the elderly would:

> *"provide an opportunity to assess the nature and scale of the problems affecting elderly people from ethnic minorities."*

Such FHSAs have gone (or are going) ahead with service development to black and minority ethnic groups on the basis of more general information now available about the likely needs of various populations. For example, a few FHSAs were collecting data or targetting action on special health risks amongst black and minority ethnic communities such as coronary heart disease and depression. Such health problems in these groups have been widely researched and documented, and their results are generally available.

Other approaches to finding out about local health need included contacts or joint action with local community groups and other agencies which provides services. One direct method is for those who are responsible for service provision to involve local people in identifying needs and priorities. This approach was being taken by at least two FHSAs.

2.17 VARIATION IN SERVICE RESPONSE BY SIZE OF TARGET POPULATION

It is sometimes argued that demographic or geographical factors underlie the varied pattern of service response to black and minority ethnic communities.

The range in the proportion of elderly population from black and minority ethnic groups and in the actual numbers in the areas selected for the study was very wide. Proportions varied from .04% to 5%, and numbers from approx 200 to 4,000 (1981 Census).

A systematic study of the relationship between size of population of black or minority ethnic elderly people and service response was not possible on the basis of this survey. Table 2b, however, shows that if FHSAs are divided into two groups in terms of population size, the response of the group with the lower population to a fixed range of items does not vary significantly from those with higher populations.

Moreover, when FHSAs are ranged in rank order of either proportion or numbers of elderly people from black and minority ethnic populations, it is immediately apparent that some of the most comprehensive and innovative service developments have been undertaken by FHSAs at the lower end of the range for both proportion and numbers. For example Derbyshire FHSA was close to the lower end of the range of both proportion and numbers within this sample. Since producing 'Raising the Issues' it has developed an annually reviewed implementation programme of measures identified. In Liverpool, where there is a long-settled black community unlikely to be included in the 1981 Census as born outside Britain, the FHSA has also been developing a pro-active community development approach to the needs of its black and minority ethnic communities.

It is also clear that there are FHSAs towards the upper end of the ranges which have taken few initiatives. The six FHSAs with the highest proportions of black and minority ethnic elderly (and generally also the highest actual numbers), however, had all taken substantial steps towards improving the level of primary health care for these communities, particularly in the development of linkworker schemes.

2.18 VARIATION IN SERVICE RESPONSE BY TYPE OF AREA

Type of area has also sometimes been considered important (Farleigh, 1990). It has been suggested that in the metropolitan inner-city areas, where black and minority ethnic populations are more concentrated, they are more 'visible' and their needs more likely to be acknowledged.

Some analysis of response by area type was carried out. Of the 44 respondents, 21 covered country areas and 23 were metropolitan areas. Both the average proportion and number of elderly black and minority ethnic people were higher in the metropolitan areas than in the counties. Average proportions in the counties and in the metropolitan districts were 0.9% and 1.5%

respectively, and average numbers were 900 and 1,295. (These figures slightly underestimate the difference between numbers in the two types of area, because of the overrepresentation of metropolitan districts among the non-responders.)

Table 2b shows the extent to which FHSAs had undertaken (or were undertaking) a range of specific measures. There is some interesting variation in response between counties and metropolitan areas, which might be worth further exploration. Slightly more metropolitan than county FHSAs had been in contact with their local authority or DHA in relation to black and minority ethnic communities, had participated in working groups, had had leaflets or posters translated or had advised GPs on race equality. Considerably higher numbers of metropolitan than county FHSAs maintained lists of interpreting services (30% and 14%), employed ethnic minority development officers (21% and 10%), or had carried out consumer surveys amongst these groups (22% and 10%). Although the trends were all in the same direction, and suggest that the metropolitan districts were taking a more proactive and focussed approach to the needs of black and minority ethnic communities, the small numbers involved mean that results should be interpreted cautiously.

Generally the similarity in the overall pattern of response of the two groups to the range of variables was as striking as the difference. In certain key variables such as numbers employing linkworkers, or in nature of future plans, there were no differences between the counties and the metropolitan district FHSAs. The only question which elicited a marked difference of response was on which elderly groups were perceived as having particular problems in access to primary health care. Of the 10 FHSAs which mentioned black and minority ethnic elderly, eight were metropolitan districts and only two were counties. This may reflect on the one hand a general concern amongst metropolitan FHSAs about the quality of care in the inner cities, and on the other an overriding concern in the shires about service access amongst elderly people in the rural areas.

The conclusion suggested by these findings and those reported in the previous section is that while demographic and geographical factors may explain some of the variation in service response amongst FHSAs, they do not account for all of it. Explanations may well be found in other historical or political factors, such as length of settlement in the area, the pattern and culture of service development in other local agencies in relation to black and minority ethnic communities, activity of local pressure groups or the possible employment of committed staff within particular FHSAs. It would be profitable to examine the possible effects and relative importance of such factors.

2.19   SUMMARY

It would appear that, in relation to services which would directly benefit elderly people from black and minority ethnic communities, FHSAs have been moving in different directions, at different rates.

Only two initiatives were reported as having been targetted specifically at elderly people from black and minority ethnic communities. Only one FHSA appeared to have directly identified and targetted resources towards specific ways of providing health checks for the over-75s amongst the black and minority ethnic population.

A significant minority of areas had made a specific commitment to the quality of primary health care for black and minority ethnic communities generally, and had taken significant service development measures. In terms of resources, the most substantial commitment lay in targetted practice improvement programmes or in the employment of specific staff in a direct service delivery or development capacity. Although such measures were not directed specifically to elderly people, they may derive some direct benefit from them. In the absence of evidence, however, this cannot be certain.

Some FHSAs had made less commitment, but were nonetheless beginning to approach the needs of black and minority ethnic groups on a broader front through liaison with statutory and voluntary agencies, joint health needs assessment exercises or one-off short-term development initiatives. No evidence was yet available to show that such initiatives were of specific benefit to elderly people.

All such initiatives, however, were of possible use in the development of services for this group if a specific focus on the elderly was included in project design. As some FHSAs pointed out, for example, the potential benefit to elderly people from black and minority ethnic groups from inter-agency collaboration over community care plans is enormous. This is an issue which it would be particularly useful to monitor over the next few years as the Commissioning Agencies develop, or to assess in a follow-up study.

A substantial minority of this sample of FHSAs had given very little or no priority at all to the question of services for black and minority ethnic communities, or any sub-group within them. There was little evidence that variation in service response was related to variation in proportion or size of local black or minority ethnic elderly population.

The majority of FHSAs were not yet exploiting their wider powers in service monitoring and training to tackle service improvement for black and minority ethnic elderly people. This will need to be taken up now through the commissioning process.

3 POSTAL SURVEY OF GENERAL PRACTITIONERS: SELECTION, RESPONSE RATES AND CHARACTERISTICS OF THE SAMPLE

3.1 OBJECTIVES OF THE POSTAL SURVEY

Whilst detailed information about services, problems of delivery, perceptions of need etc. could only be explored in face-to-face interviews, there was a need first to obtain a general picture of primary health care provision for elderly people from black and minority ethnic groups in different areas across England and Wales. This could be carried out most cost-effectively by means of a postal survey of relevant general practitioners. The main objectives of the postal survey were to obtain basic information about:

- the extent of general practitioner involvement with elderly people from black and minority groups in areas with significant proportions of people from these groups;
- any specific approaches or methods used in general practice for assessment and treatment of elderly people from these groups;
- perceptions among general practitioners of any problems in the assessment and treatment of elderly people from these groups.

3.2 SELECTION OF THE SAMPLES

It was therefore necessary to obtain a sample of general practitioners from areas in England and Wales with varying characteristics and with different proportions of elderly people from black and ethnic minorities on their lists. As discussed, although GPFHs have extra scope for targetting resources at patient need, they were not treated separately within this survey.

There was no straightforward way of achieving a sample. General information on the number of black and minority ethnic elderly people on individual GP lists is not available. One approach would have been to sample heavily on a random basis within a small number of wards known to have large black and minority ethnic communities. Such information, however, would have been unable to indicate the national situation, because of the considerable local variation in service provision for minority groups. On the other hand, the resources of the project did not permit a large random sample from a wide range of areas, which would anyway have entailed the inclusion in the survey of many respondents with none of the target patients at all, and little immediate experience of the issues.

The following method was therefore adopted.

1 As with the survey described in Chapter 2, FHSAs in England and Wales whose populations (according to the 1981 Census) included 1500 or more people aged 45 years and over whose place of birth suggested they were from black or minority ethnic groups were selected (55 out of the total of 98 FHSAs). Although this was necessarily an arbitrary cut-off point it ensured that all the main areas of black and minority ethnic group residence were included, as well as a few less well identified areas.

2   These 55 FHSAs were then ranked according to their percentage of
    people from black and minority ethnic groups of pensionable age (1981
    Census). They were divided into three bands of approximately equal size,
    and five FHSAs were selected at random from each band. The fact that
    the black and minority ethnic population in this country has settled
    largely in clusters in the inner cities, particularly in London, meant that
    the FHSA areas included in these three bands fell into roughly three
    types. The band of areas at the lower end of the scale consisted mainly of
    the metropolitan districts with dense localised but fairly small popu-
    lations, the middle band consisted largely of counties with smaller more
    dispersed pockets of black and minority ethnic population, and the third
    band was mainly London Boroughs with some of the largest black and
    minority ethnic communities in the country.

3   The total number of general practitioners for all 15 FHSAs was calcu-
    lated, and names and addresses obtained. This provided the initial
    sampling frame, which—using a sampling interval of eight—allowed the
    selection of a sample of approximately 600. This was considerable higher
    than the expected achieved sample in order to allow for non-response.

4   The actual selection of general practitioners was however not purely
    random since this might have led to the selection of many who had few
    (if any) patients from among black and minority ethnic elders. Each
    FHSA was contacted and asked, if possible, to identify from among their
    general practitioners, those with significant numbers of patients from
    black and minority ethnic groups. Approximately half the eventual
    sample of GPs was randomly selected from those selected by FHSAs and
    half from those not pre-selected by the FHSAs.

Since the basis of the sample was size of elderly black and minority ethnic
population by area, much of the analysis of the data was focussed on the
characteristics of respondents by the three area bands. It is reasonable to
assume, however, that the information obtained provides a fairly representative picture of primary care provision for the majority of black and minority
ethnic elderly people. The sample was targetted towards the main areas of
settlement, and within these areas focussed on those GPs most likely to serve
local black and minority ethnic populations. For this reason some analysis has
also been carried out on results for the sample as a whole.

For convenience of reference throughout this report the three bands of FHSA
areas on which the survey is based have been named in accordance with their
broad characteristics. The first band of areas with the lowest proportions of
elderly black and minority ethnic populations and consisting mainly of
Metropolitan areas outside London is referred to as 'non-London metropolitan areas', the middle band of county areas is called 'counties', and the
third band of mainly London Boroughs with large elderly black and minority
ethnic populations is called 'London Boroughs'.

3.3 RESPONSE RATES

A questionnaire was sent to 590 GPs, of whom 284 were in Sample 1 (those pre-identified by FHSAs as likely to have significant numbers of patients from black and minority ethnic groups) and 306 were in Sample 2 (those not so identified by FHSAs). Two weeks later a follow-up mailing was sent to non-responders. Two to four weeks after that outstanding non-responders were telephoned.

A number of GPs were established as ineligible through changes in employment, retirement, moving, long-term sickness or leave, or through having no elderly patients from black and minority ethnic groups (see Table 3a). (Twelve GPs who said they had no relevant patients at present, but who had done so in the past, and completed the questionnaire, were retained in the effective sample).

Table 3a: Type of response by area

	Non-London metropolitan No.	County No.	London Boroughs No.	Total No.
Total GPs mailed	240	122	228	590
Found to be ineligible:				
– GP moved, retired, etc.	8	4	5	17
– no target population	25	12	3	40
Questionnaire returned:				
– fully completed	114	58	108	280
– incomplete: no relevant info.	1	1	3	5
no time	8	6	7	21
no reason given	4	2	4	10
Questionnaire not returned	80	39	98	217
Response rates:				
– Fully or partially completed questionnaires as % of those assumed eligible*	61%	63%	55%	59%
– Fully completed questionnaires as percentage of those assumed eligible*	55%	55%	49%	53%

* It should be noted that the total assumed eligible probably includes further ineligible respondents, but for whom confirmation of this fact was unobtainable because they did not return the questionnaire.

The response rate (excluding those who responded but were ineligible) was 59%. This was considered good; postal surveys in general are unlikely to achieve very high response rates, and postal surveys of general practitioners experience particular difficulty. Several specific factors affected this survey, and these are detailed below.

1 Almost half of the questionnaires were posted to GPs not expected to have many patients in the group targetted by the survey. (Indeed, because the black and minority ethnic population tends to be clustered, and because some of the sub-groups within it have a relatively young age structure, many GPs were unlikely to have any of the target patients at all.) The results shown in Table 3b undoubtedly under-report this factor.

2 Another factor which was expected to affect the response rate was the timing of the survey: it was carried out during the first year of implementation of the new contract when many GPs were under considerable pressure. This was exacerbated by the fact that the survey coincided with the end of the financial year. Some of those who refused indicated that pressure on time was an important reason.

3 A further factor which appeared to influence response was a reluctance to give subjective estimates of practice population data, in the absence of up-to-date information systems. Some respondents refused to complete the questionnaire on the grounds that they did not have the information requested, even though the accompanying letter had stressed that respondents were not expected to have complete information on some of the issues covered.

The response rate in the London Boroughs was somewhat lower than in the other areas. This was rather surprising as interest in the study might have been expected to be highest here. There are several factors which might explain it: the particular pressure of work in the inner London Boroughs, the large proportion of single-handed GPs, and poorer access to information because of the lower proportion of practices with age-sex registers.

Table 3b: Type of response by sample

	Sample 1 No.	Sample 2 No.
Total GPs mailed	284	306
Found to be ineligible	16	41
Questionnaire fully completed	148	132
Fully completed questionnaires as % of those assumed eligible	55%	50%

The proportion of fully completed questionnaires was considerably higher amongst Sample 1 respondents (those pre-identified by FHSAs as eligible) than those in Sample 2 (not pre-identified by FHSAs). This was not surprising, since numbers of black and minority ethnic patients were lower in the latter sample.

3.4 PROPORTION OF BLACK AND MINORITY ETHNIC ELDERLY PEOPLE ON PRACTICE LISTS IN SAMPLES 1 AND 2

As outlined above (Section 3.1), FHSAs were asked to identify GPs likely to have significant numbers of elderly black and minority ethnic patients: samples were drawn randomly both from those who had been identified and those who had not.

The samples can be compared by examining answers to the question about how many patients in the practice list aged 65 and over were from black and ethnic minorities. As is reported below, very few GPs routinely recorded ethnic origin; it is therefore not surprising that a large proportion of respondents (108, 39%) said they did not know and most of the figures given are estimates.

Responses were grouped into fairly broad bands to avoid over-reliance on actual figures quoted. A predictable spread of responses emerged (See Table 3c). This lent credibility to the estimates and enabled further analyses on the basis of numbers to be carried out.

How far did these results confirm the 'two-sample' model? Table 3d shows the number of patients in the target groups for the two samples.

Table 3c: Numbers of black and minority ethnic over-65s on practice list

	All respondents	
	No.	%
None at present	12	7
1–10	74	43
11–50	39	23
51–100	17	10
101–200	15	9
201 and over	15	9
Total giving numbers (base for %)	172	101
Not known	108	
Total respondents	280	

Table 3d: Number of target patients by sample

| | Sample 1 | | Sample 2 | |
	No.	%	No.	%
None at present	–	–	11	12
1–10	28	36	46	49
11–50	17	22	22	23
More than 50	33	42	15	16
Total giving numbers (base for %)	78	100	94	100
Not known	70		38	
Total respondents	148		132	

As this shows, a higher proportion of Sample 1 than Sample 2 (47% of the total as against 29%) said that they did not know the number. This may be because where numbers were higher it was more difficult to make an estimate. Of those who could give an answer, as expected more GPs in Sample 1 reported high numbers of target patients than in Sample 2. There was considerable overlap, however, with 16% of Sample 2 saying that they had more than fifty patients from the target population. This shows that while FHSAs were reasonably able to identify those GPs with markedly higher numbers of target patients, there was a margin of inaccuracy. The distribution of such patients between practices appeared much wider than anticipated. The results suggest that many more GPs may be dealing with elderly black or minority ethnic patients than is realised by FHSAs.

These results support the decision not to sample only from those GPs who had been identified as having a high number of target patients. The method used achieved its objective of constructing a stratified sample of GPs, slightly weighted towards those with higher numbers of the target patients (see section 3.1).

3.5 CHARACTERISTICS OF SAMPLE PRACTICES BY AREA

GP respondents and their practices in the three types of area were examined and compared for a range of standard characteristics usually regarded as important in relation to the delivery of primary health care at the practice level. As noted earlier, GPFHs were not treated separately.

Results demonstrate significant differences between the three types of area in the nature of the patient populations and the likely demand for primary health care, the way in which primary health care was delivered, and in the range of services offered to patients. As will be shown, these differences have important implications for the care available to groups of elderly people from black or ethnic minorities.

3.5.1 Numbers of target patients in each type of area

Many more GP respondents in London Boroughs reported having more than 50 elderly patients from black or minority ethnic groups on their lists: 27 respondents, compared with 14 (non-London metropolitan areas) and seven (counties). These results are consistent with the original banding of FHSAs by number and proportion of patients (see section 3.1).

Interestingly, however, figures for the counties are lower than for non-London metropolitan areas, although the FHSAs included in the counties had higher numbers and proportions of the target client group than those in non-London metropolitan areas. Several of the results presented in this report will show greater similarities between non-London metropolitan areas and London Boroughs, than between London Boroughs and the counties.

3.5.2 Proportion of elderly patients on practice lists

Very few GP respondents in any type of area recorded proportions of elderly patients higher than 20%, and 2 out of 5 were no higher than 10%. There was, however, some variation by type of area; county respondents had slightly lower proportions of elderly people than the others, and non-London metropolitan areas had considerably more practices with more than 20% (See Table 3e).

Table 3e: Approximate proportion of all patients aged 65 and over on practice lists, by area

	Non-London metropolitan		County		London Boroughs	
	No.	%	No.	%	No.	%
Don't know	5	4	1	2	9	8
10% or under	43	38	28	50	45	42
11–20%	45	40	25	45	43	40
21–30%	16	14	2	3	8	7
More than 30%	4	4	–	–	2	2
Total respondents answering question (base for %)	113	100	56	100	107	99

3.5.3 Practice staff

Whether GP respondents had a Practice Manager or Practice Nurse was also examined (Table 3f). A higher proportion of non-London metropolitan and county respondents had access to a practice nurse than London Borough respondents, and those in London Boroughs were also least likely to have a Practice Manager.

Table 3f: Practices with (i) a Manager, (ii) access to a Practice Nurse

	Non-London metropolitan %	County %	London Boroughs %
Practice Manager	65	73	51
Access to Practice Nurse	91	88	76

3.5.4 Practice size
Table 3g examines the number of doctors in the practice. It reveals significant differences by area. The proportion of respondents working single-handed was twice as high in London Boroughs, and one and a half times as high in the counties, as the proportion in non-London metropolitan areas.

3.5.5 Location of practice base
In line with this, many more practices in non-London metropolitan areas (38%) were in health centres than were those in the counties (29%) or London Boroughs (27%).

Table 3g: Number of general practitioners in practice, by type of area

	Non-London metropolitan No.	%	County No.	%	London Boroughs No.	%
Single-handed	21	18	18	31	39	36
2 doctors	36	31	11	19	29	27
3 doctors	26	23	7	12	16	15
4 doctors	17	15	8	14	12	11
5 and over	14	13	14	24	12	11
Total respondents	114	100	58	100	108	100

Table 3h: Provision of health promotion clinics. by type of area

	Non-London metropolitan No.	%	County No.	%	London Boroughs No.	%
Asthma clinic	64	64	29	54	59	68
Diabetes clinic	68	68	37	69	70	80
Hypertension clinic	74	74	40	74	67	77
Well-women clinic	91	91	53	98	84	97
Well-men clinic	71	71	48	89	73	84
Total respondents answering question (base for %s)	100		54		87	

3.5.6 Provision of health promotion clinics

GP respondents were asked whether their practice ran any clinics. As Table 3h shows, provision was high in all areas.

3.5.7 Availability of age/sex registers

More GP respondents in non-London metropolitan areas (65%) and the counties (76%) had computerised age/sex registers than did those in London Boroughs (55%).

3.5.8 Receipt of deprivation allowance

There were wide discrepancies between areas; an almost negligible number of GP respondents in the counties received deprivation payments, while 67% of the non-London metropolitan sample and 78% of respondents in the London Boroughs were receiving them.

3.5.9 Ethnic origin of GP respondents

Table 3i shows that the ethnic composition of the sample varied by area: a considerably lower proportion of the non-London metropolitan respondents were of Asian origin, and a considerably higher proportion were of white UK origin. The proportion of respondents of black or minority ethnic origin was highest in the London Boroughs (more than 50%), where the highest proportion of such patients was also to be found.

Table 3i: Ethnic origin of GP respondents, by area

	Non-London metropolitan		County		London Boroughs	
	No.	%	No.	%	No.	%
White UK	74	65	30	52	43	40
African	3	3	–	–	2	2
Asian	32	28	25	43	46	43
Chinese	1	1	–	–	5	5
Other	4	3	–	–	6	5
Not stated	–	–	3	5	6	5
Total respondents answering question	114	100	58	100	108	100

3.5.10 Sex of GP respondents

The vast majority of doctors were male, but the non-London metropolitan areas had a much higher proportion of woman doctors.

Table 3j: Sex of GP respondents, by area

	Non-London metropolitan		County		London Boroughs	
	No.	%	No.	%	No.	%
Male	78	70	47	84	91	85
Female	34	30	9	16	16	15
Total respondents answering question	112	100	56	100	107	100

3.5.11 Main black and minority ethnic group seen by GP respondents

GP respondents were asked simply to record the main ethnic groups from which most of their elderly black and minority patients came. Again striking differences between types of area can be seen. For example, a higher proportion of respondents in the London Boroughs reported Afro-Caribbean patients as their main elderly black or minority ethnic group. This reflects the clustering of this population in the London Boroughs and in a few other major urban areas. Indian groups were more likely to be mentioned by respondents in the counties than in the other two areas; and respondents in the non-London metropolitan area were more likely to mention Pakistani groups.

Table 3k: Main black or minority ethnic groups seen by GP respondents, by area

	Non-London metropolitan		County		London Boroughs	
	No.	%	No.	%	No.	%
Afro-Caribbean	52	48	15	26	73	68
Indian	46	43	39	68	55	51
Pakistani	56	52	24	42	46	43
Bangladeshi	19	18	6	11	32	30
Chinese	24	22	7	12	22	20
Central & Southern African	12	11	1	2	22	20
North African/Arab	1	1	–	–	–	–
Vietnamese	1	1	–	–	1	1
Other	11	10	5	9	12	11
Total respondents answering question (base for %)	108		57		108	

NB: Percentages add to more than 100 because most respondents mentioned more than one main group

3.5.12 Comparison of respondent's ethnic origin with that of patients

There was a small, though not significant, association between the ethnic origin of the GP respondent and the ethnic group which formed his or her main minority ethnic patient group; a somewhat higher percentage of Asian GPs had Asians as their main minority group (61%) than did white GPs (51%). The white GPs were concomitantly more likely to cite Afro-Caribbeans or other black or minority ethnic groups.

3.6 SUMMARY OF SAMPLE CHARACTERISTICS

The findings reported in this chapter show some of the basic characteristics of the practices in this sample within which primary care for elderly people from black and minority ethnic groups is delivered. They show that in this sample of general practitioners (drawn from areas in which at the 1981 Census the population consisted of 1,500 or more people aged 45 or over from black and minority ethnic groups) almost all had some elderly patients from these groups; 50% of those who could cite a figure had more than ten such patients, and 28% had more than fifty. The main group served was Asian, then Afro-Caribbean. The proportion of GP respondents who were themselves from black or minority ethnic groups was high (46%).

There were some striking differences in sample characteristics, particularly between the London Boroughs and the other areas. Although such comparisons were not a primary aim of this survey these area differences are interesting and important. The London Borough practices had by far the highest proportion of elderly patients from black and minority ethnic groups (48% of GPs saying they had 50 or more as against less than 20% of the GPs in the other areas). They had the highest proportion of GPs who were themselves from black or minority ethnic groups (55%), and, along with the counties, fewer women doctors. The London Borough practices were also less likely to have a practice manager, more likely to be single-handed practices, less likely to be based in a Health Centre, less likely to have a computerised age/sex register. Most strikingly, perhaps, the GPs in the London Boroughs (though followed quite closely by those in the non-London metropolitan areas) were overwhelmingly likely to receive deprivation allowances (78% compared with only 9% of those in the counties); this indicates the high levels of need in these areas.

The results of this survey are consistent with evidence from other sources that the majority of elderly people from black or ethnic minorities receive primary health care in areas where there are the highest levels of need, in practices where the range of resources available is most limited, and which, because of their small size, are unlikely to be able to use the provisions within the White Paper on general practice (Department of Health, 1990) to expand their services.

The results also suggest that the key problems of primary health care in the inner city which the Acheson Report (1988) identified and targetted for specific action still affect the care received by many elderly people from black or minority ethnic communities. These doctors are carrying the burden of care in the most stressful areas. The extent to which the extra resources which have been made available are appropriately targetted, or sufficient for them to provide this care, needs continuous assessment. As the Fundholding Scheme expands, any impact on services for this patient group will need to be evaluated.

4 POSTAL SURVEY OF GENERAL PRACTITIONERS: THE FINDINGS

This chapter describes the main findings of the GP postal survey.

4.1 RECORDING ETHNIC ORIGIN

Only 14% of the GP respondents recorded the ethnic origin of their patients routinely, with a further 17% recording on an *ad hoc* basis.

Table 4a: Whether ethnic origin of patients recorded

	Total		Non-London metropolitan		County		London Borough	
	No.	%	No.	%	No.	%	No.	%
Yes	38	14	15	13	5	9	18	17
No	194	69	79	69	43	74	72	67
Sometimes	48	17	20	18	10	17	18	17
Total respondents	280	100	114	100	58	100	108	101

The proportion of respondents recording ethnic origin routinely was highest in the London Boroughs, where nearly twice as many were recorded as in the counties. Even here, however, only one-sixth did so routinely. The survey did not attempt to assess the quality or usefulness of the way in which this information was collected, although this issue is equally important, because little routine recording was anticipated.

GP respondents were also asked if they kept any other information on the ethnic composition of the patient population they served, and only 34 (12%) said they did. Such information consisted mainly of Census or other aggregate data on the ethnic composition of local populations.

The practice population is the basic unit for primary health care planning and resource allocation. Information on the composition of general practice populations will become increasingly important to local needs assessment, and the effective representation of different groups of patients at the strategic level. These results show that routine recording of ethnic origin is not widespread among general practitioners. Interestingly, however, the practice is higher in London Boroughs and other metropolitan areas where the black and minority ethnic populations are clustered and GPs have higher proportions on their lists. In such areas perhaps there is a greater awareness of need related to ethnicity. The practice of recording was not related to the ethnic origin of the GP respondent.

Respondents' views on recording ethnic origin were further explored in the interviews, and are reported later. Most respondents only recorded where an individual need had been perceived, and very few saw it as useful for more general and routine data collection purposes.

4.2 COMMUNICATION AND THE USE OF INTERPRETERS

The survey looked in some detail at the question of 'communication' in primary health care. Most studies have shown poor knowledge or under-standing of English amongst particular groups of elderly people from black or ethnic minorities. The issues which arise where service providers and patients do not share the same language and culture have been widely regarded as a key barrier to access to health and other welfare services for these groups.

Recent recommendations have focussed on the need to overcome this within primary health care through methods such as the provision of appropriate interpreting services, employment of staff who speak a range of languages, and the appointment of linkworkers or facilitators. Recent policy changes have made provision for the employment of such staff at practice level.

The survey sought to establish the extent to which difficulties in communi-cation with any elderly people from black or ethnic minorities were being experienced, the ways in which primary health carers dealt with the situation and their views on these issues.

4.2.1 Frequency of consultations with non-English speaking patients

The vast majority (214, 76%) of GP respondents reported that they were consulted by elderly patients who did not speak English. Although the frequency of such consultations varied considerably, for many respondents it was a weekly occurrence. Over one-third of respondents in the London Boroughs saw such patients weekly, as did 30% in non-London metropolitan areas and 24% in the counties.

Table 4b: Frequency of consultation by elderly patients who do not speak English, for white and Asian GP respondents

	White UK		Asian	
	No.	%	No.	%
Not at all	36	25	13	13
Less than once per week	80	55	33	32
About once per week	9	6	17	17
A few times per week	14	10	20	19
Nearly every day/every day	4	3	14	14
Don't know	2	1	5	5
Not applicable	1	1	1	1
Total respondents (base for %)	146	101	103	101

NB: Respondents who were neither White UK nor Asian or who did not state their ethnic origin are excluded from this and similar tables

Table 4b shows that Asian respondents were much more likely to see patients who did not speak English than those of white UK origin. This finding is consistent with other studies (Ahmad et al, 1988). Thirty-three per cent of Asian respondents saw elderly patients who did not speak English a few times per week or more, compared with 13% of those of white UK origin. This was a statistically significant difference ($\chi^2 = 5.54$, DF[1], $p < .05$). While these figures suggest that many patients overcome linguistic and cultural barriers within primary health care through choice of GP, nonetheless 13% of the white UK respondents were seeing elderly patients who could not speak English a few times per week or more.

4.2.2 Main methods of dealing with communication issues
Consistent with other studies, the main source of help reported was the patient's family. This was true of all types of area, and was particularly common in the London Boroughs.

Not surprisingly, Asian doctors reported much less reliance on family members than white UK respondents (36% and 54% respectively). Where Asian respondents could not rely on their own language skills, however, reliance on family members was the biggest single source of help. Slightly more white UK respondents said they got help from interpreters and linkworkers as a

4c: Main methods of dealing with communication issues, by type of area

	Total		Non-London metropolitan		County		London Borough	
	No.	%	No.	%	No.	%	No.	%
problems/Never arisen	73	27	33	29	19	33	21	20
ly member helps	132	48	50	44	23	40	59	56
sign language/chart	14	5	7	6	3	5	4	4
worker (inc. practice	8	3	7	6	–	–	1	1
ondent speaks								
age	21	8	3	3	7	12	11	10
er helps	10	4	4	4	2	4	4	4
e helps	2	1	–	–	1	2	1	1
ptionist helps	12	4	4	4	2	4	6	6
preters used	44	16	20	18	4	7	20	19
nt volunteers	1	–	1	1	–	–	–	–
er	12	4	7	6	2	4	3	3
respondents ering question for %)	275		113		57		105	

Percentages add to more than 100 because some respondents gave more than one answer main method (20% and 15% respectively), although overall Asian respondents made more use of formal interpreting services than white UK respondents (see Section 4.2.5). More Asian respondents said they used receptionists and sign language as main methods, although numbers are very small indeed.

Table 4d: Usual methods of dealing with communication issues, for white UK and Asian GP respondents

	White UK		Asian	
	No.	%	No.	%
No problems/Never arisen	43	30	24	24
Family member helps	78	54	37	36
Use sign language/chart	3	2	8	8
Linkworkers (inc. practice link)	5	3	3	3
Respondent speaks language	–	–	19	19
Partner helps	4	3	3	3
Nurse helps	1	1	1	1
Receptionist helps	5	3	5	5
Interpreters used	24	17	12	12
Patient volunteers	1	1	–	–
Other	7	5	4	4
Total respondents answering question (base for %)	145		102	

NB: Percentages add to more than 100 because some respondents gave more than one answer

4.2.3 Family members as interpreter

Considerable dissatisfaction with the use of family members as interpreter in consultations was recorded (Table 4e). Inaccurate translation and embarrassment were the main perceived problems. Recording of problems was much higher in the London Boroughs and other metropolitan areas than in the counties. Overall 45% of GP respondents recorded problems in using family members as interpreters.

As Table 4f shows, white UK and Asian GP respondents reported the same range of dissatisfactions with family members as interpreters. Reporting of such issues, however, was generally much lower amongst Asian respondents, who were also more likely to think that there were no difficulties at all. It is likely that Asian respondents were more able to handle any linguistic and cultural issues which arose, because of their broader linguistic and cultural compatibility. More white UK respondents reported problems with inaccuracy, consultation time, subjectivity, embarrassment and confidentiality. The differences between the two groups were statistically significant in relation to embarrassment ($\chi^2 = 3.93$, DF^1, $p < .05$) and inaccuracy ($\chi^2 = 4.38$, DF^1, $p < .05$).

It is clear that while respondents rely heavily on family members when they do not speak their patient's language, they often find it an inappropriate and less than satisfactory source of help, and feel that the quality of the consultation is sometimes compromised. This was further explored in the interviews, where many remarks vividly illustrated the shortcomings of this approach (see Chapter 6). Commentators have dismissed the use of relatives as an appropriate source of interpreting help (Fewster, 1989; Richter et al, 1979).

Table 4e: Problems with family/friends as interpreter, by type of area

	Non-London metropolitan		County		London Borough	
	No.	%	No.	%	No.	%
Inaccuracy	27	24	10	18	24	23
Length of consultation	10	9	2	4	9	9
Subjective interpreting	4	4	1	2	20	19
Embarrassment	21	19	1	10	11	10
Confidentiality	9	8	6	11	7	7
Availability of help	1	1	2	4	5	5
Don't know	32	28	22	39	17	16
None	32	28	13	23	36	34
Other	3	3	4	7	1	1
Total respondents answering question (base for %)	113		56		105	

NB: Percentages add to more than 100 because some respondents gave more than one answer

Table 4f: Problems with family/friends as interpreter, for white UK and Asian GP respondents

	White UK		Asian	
	No.	%	No.	%
Inaccuracy	38	26	15	15
Length of consultation	10	7	8	8
Subjective interpreting	14	10	8	8
Embarrassment	21	14	7	7
Confidentiality	15	10	6	6
Availability of help	1	1	4	4
Don't know	40	28	26	26
None	35	24	38	38
Other	6	4	–	–
Total respondents answering question (base for %)	145		100	

NB: Percentages add to more than 100 because some respondents gave more than one answer

In addition to the open question about the main methods used in dealing with communication issues, the survey sought information on a fixed range of other methods, such as the employment of the skills of other staff, and the use of formal interpreting services.

4.2.4 Practice staff as interpreters

As anticipated, the practice team itself was a significant resource for help with interpreting, and Table 4g shows the extent of this.

Table 4g: Interpreting help received from practice staff

	Non-London metropolitan		County		London Borough	
	No.	%	No.	%	No.	%
None	87	76	49	84	72	68
Partner	8	7	4	7	12	11
Practice manager	2	2	–	–	4	4
Receptionist/secretary	16	14	5	9	26	25
Practice nurse	4	3	1	2	4	4
Health visitor/District nurse	2	2	1	2	3	3
Other	2	2	–	–	–	–
Total respondents (base for %)	114		58		106	

NB: Percentages add to more than 100 because some respondents gave more than one answer

Very much higher numbers reported making some use of practice staff as interpreters than had recorded this as a main method of dealing with communication issues. For example, while 47 GP respondents said their receptionist provided help, only twelve had recorded this as a main method. Twenty-four said that they got help from their practice partners, while only ten had recorded this as a main method.

4.2.5 Employment of staff to work with patients from black or minority ethnic groups

GP respondents were asked whether they employed any practice staff primarily to work with patients from black or minority ethnic groups. Table 4h shows that this was very uncommon, with 84% saying they did not employ any staff for this purpose.

The results show that where primary health care staff are employed specifically for black or minority ethnic communities, they are likely to be practice partners. The other main staff group were receptionists; twelve were said to have been employed specifically, but numbers reported to be interpreting, as noted above, are higher than this. Other staff groups were barely represented.

Table 4h: Employment of practice staff primarily to work with black or minority ethnic patients

| | Non-London metropolitan | | County | | London Borough | |
	No.	%	No.	%	No.	%
None/NA	90	80	53	95	87	83
Practice partners	11	10	1	2	13	12
Receptionists	9	8	2	4	8	8
Practice nurses	2	2	–	–	6	6
Health visitors	3	3	2	4	8	1
Other (Interp/link)	4	4	–	–	1	1
Total respondents (base for %)	113		56		105	

NB: Need for health education and promotion services for elderly people from black and minority ethnic groups

4.2.6 Need for health education and promotion services for elderly people from black and minority ethnic groups

The potential demand for such services is explored in the interviews. One question, however, was included in the postal questionnaire. GP respondents were asked directly how helpful increased access to a linkworker or special nurse to give health information/education/promotion would be.

Sixty per cent of respondents in the London Boroughs said it would be helpful or very helpful. This compared with 47% in non-London metropolitan areas and 35% in the counties. These figures point to a significant perception of service need, which is greatest in the areas with the highest proportions of black and minority ethnic elderly patients.

These responses may reflect the slightly lower access to practice nurses recorded in the London Boroughs, as well as a greater awareness of patient need. They draw attention to the fact that the health care of elderly people may be impaired not only by mismatches of language or culture, but also by a lack of health education and health awareness. This is a problem they share with elderly people from the indigenous population.

4.2.7 Other approaches – interpreters/linkworkers/advocates

A number of different posts have been developed which offer interpretation (amongst other primary health care services) to black and minority ethnic patients. The job title varies depending on the particular focus of the service offered; examples include 'linkworker', 'advocate', 'health liaison officer'. A multiple-choice question was asked to try to identify which sources of formal interpreting help were most significant within primary health care.

Results are shown separately for the different types of service. Caution should be used in interpreting the figures since it was apparent from the interviews that GP respondents were often unclear about the type of worker used and the source of funding.

Table 4i: Use of interpreters, linkworkers and advocates, by source of funding/ employment

	FHSA full/joint funding No.	DHA full/joint funding No.	LA full/joint funding No.	Voluntary No.	Practice employed No.
Interpreters	9	7	7	16	10
Linkworkers	13	9	7	1	4
Advocates	4	0	2	7	2

Note: Some of the GP respondents used interpreting help from more than one source, and so will appear more than once on the tables. It cannot be assumed that respondents focussed only on services used in relation to elderly people.

As was reported at the beginning of this section, 214 (76%) of all GP respondents reported seeing elderly patients who did not speak English. While some of these patients have doctors who speak their own language, only 22% of the GP respondents said that they never experienced communication difficulties. In spite of this, it appears that formal services play a limited role in helping with interpretation at practice level.

Numbers have not been broken down by type of area because they are so small. Slightly more Asian than white UK respondents reported using interpreting services, but the small numbers mean this has to be treated with caution. It does suggest, however, that in spite of being able to make use of their own language skills, Asian doctors are nonetheless responsible for the care of a range of patients from black or minority ethnic groups whose language they do not know.

A low level of use of such services has been found in other studies (Wright, 1983; Ahmed et al, 1989), and dependence on the doctor's own skills and on family members have been given as reasons. In answer to a question about any difficulties with formal interpreting services, it was clear that availability was a major issue. Thirty-three of the 46 respondents who gave details of problems mentioned lack of availability. Half of these respondents came from the London Boroughs, where the need is presumed to be greatest.

Other problems got few mentions: those raised were scarce resources to pay for services, the difficulty of organising times which suited all parties, lack of health expertise, and longer consultations. Twenty-two respondents said there were no problems.

However, when interpreting services were discussed in the interviews (see Chapter 6) it became apparent that GP respondents had often been dissatisfied with them, and had reservations about their use. Difficulty in finding appropriately skilled or qualified interpreters has been cited in other studies (e.g. Ebden, 1988).

4.2.8 Availability of translated printed materials
In spite of the fact that just over three-quarters of the sample reported having consultations with elderly people who did not speak English, only 40% of the GP respondents overall said that translated resources were available for elderly people in their practices. Availability was greatest in the London Boroughs (48%), compared with 40% in the non-London metropolitan areas and 25% in the counties. Respondents of Asian origin were more likely to provide translated materials than those of white UK origin (53% and 42% respectively).

Only 36% of respondents overall reported that their local DHA provided translated materials, and only 24% said that their local social service department made provision of this kind. These results probably reflect a lack of knowledge of what was available as well as a lack of appropriate provision. As is shown later in the report, GP knowledge of any specific local services was patchy.

Comments made in interviews indicated both a lack of faith in the value of translated materials to elderly people (many of whom might not be literate in their mother-tongue) and a lack of material on appropriate topics. The higher use of translated materials in the London Boroughs, and by GPs of Asian origin, suggested that there is a need for them and that they should be more widely available within primary care services. Good local inventories of available resources would be useful for dissemination of information as well as providing a basis for audit of materials and the identification of any gaps.

4.2.9 Communication: summary
There is a scarcity of data on how the quality of communication between health professionals and the elderly indigenous population compares with that experienced by elderly people from different ethnic and racial backgrounds. The extent to which communication difficulties are related to any underuse of services is unknown; it has been suggested that the significance of language and cultural differences in restricting access to appropriate health care has been overestimated (Ahmad, 1989).

The findings reported above, however, show that communication issues are widespread. The importance to patients of being able to communicate with their general practitioners has been shown in other studies, although these did not focus specifically on elderly people (Ahmed et al, 1989). This survey shows that high numbers of GP respondents regularly see patients with whom they cannot communicate well, and that many of the methods employed to deal with this are far from satisfactory.

Many of the methods employed to overcome communication problems may involve a compromise in standards. Primary health care consultations for elderly people who do not speak English may lack privacy and confidentiality because of the presence of close family or other people; they may be inaccurate because of their own limited linguistic expertise or that of their families or interpreters; they may only be able to convey the most rudimentary information because of dependence on sign language; they may contain mutual misunderstandings; or the presence of strangers or children may inhibit full self-expression. Consultations on more intimate physical or mental health problems are likely to be least satisfactory, and this may particularly affect women.

The extent to which the importance of such factors is discounted where elderly people are concerned would be worth further exploration. One respondent commented that factors such as privacy and confidentiality were less important for elderly people because 'they have nothing to hide'.

Elderly patients from black and minority ethnic groups may overcome some of these problems by giving priority to shared linguistic and cultural background in choice of GP, but this means that their power as consumers is constrained. Other factors such as the range of services offered by the practice, the sex of the doctor (Ahmed et al, 1989), the doctor's attitude and even skills may be given less priority.

Acceptance, whether implicit or explicit, that patients from black and minority ethnic groups should see doctors from similar groups implies a 'separatist' approach to the provision of primary health care. Clearly it has some advantages for the patient; as noted earlier, patients value a shared linguistic and cultural background. Evidence from the survey suggests that there may be some particular benefits for elderly people. GP respondents were asked whether they ever discussed issues related to the ethnic background of their patients within the practice team. While almost equal proportions of Asian and white UK respondents said they did (45% and 48% respectively), a further question on whether these discussions ever related specifically to elderly people revealed striking differences: 31% of Asian compared with 11% of white UK respondents had discussed the specific needs of elderly people. In addition to this Asian respondents, as described above, were more likely to provide translated materials.

These findings may be partly a reflection of the greater involvement of Asian GPs with Asian elderly people. Only one-tenth of those respondents seeing elderly patients who could not speak English less than once a week had discussed their needs within the practice, compared with a half of those seeing such patients every day. A referring GP may be the main or only link between an elderly non-English speaking patient and the other services and may be in demand to provide interpreting and cultural liaison. The potential demands on a general practitioner with many patients who cannot speak English are great.

The other major risk for elderly people who cannot speak English is greatly restricted access to health education, promotion, screening and preventive care at primary health care level. This may be due to a lack of appropriate staff, a lack of prior health education, inappropriate or non-existent printed and visual material, or a failure of service providers to acknowledge poor standards of literacy. This was explored in greater detail in the interview study.

There are no easy answers to these difficulties. It is important that those delivering services acknowledge how the quality of consultation with some elderly people may be compromised. Other means might be used to compensate for shortcomings, such as the provision of appropriate nurse back-up, good printed or audio or audio-visual material, specially trained linkworkers, health visitors with appropriate languages, or interpreters and, if necessary, extra time with the patient. Such services do not necessarily have to be available for every consultation, but could be provided in relation to the patient's general need.

4.3 ACCESS TO FEMALE DOCTORS BY ELDERLY FEMALE PATIENTS

Some GP respondents mentioned female modesty as a particular difficulty in examining elderly people from black and minority ethnic groups (see section 4.4). The importance of access to female doctors for some women from black and minority ethnic communities has been widely documented. Table 3j showed that the proportion of female GP respondents in the London Boroughs, where there were the highest numbers and proportions of the target patients, was particularly low. There is no reason to attribute this to lower response rates amongst women in this area. The finding is consistent with the high proportion of single-handed Asian practitioners in this area. It indicates that older women in these areas have particular difficulty in gaining access to a female GP.

An open question was asked on what would happen in the respondent's practice if an elderly woman was reluctant to be examined by a male doctor (Table 4j). The results confirm that elderly female patients in the London Boroughs are less likely to be able to see a female partner, and more likely to have to be transferred to another practice, referred to a practice nurse or transferred to other services such as hospitals or clinics. Reflecting the high proportion of single-handed male doctors, Asian respondents were much less likely than white UK respondents to transfer a female patient to a female partner (38% compared with 64%). This difference was highly significant (χ^2 = 16.04, DF[1], p < .0001). They were also more likely to transfer to hospital and clinic, or to a practice nurse.

Table 4j: Action taken by GP respondent on refusal by elderly woman to be examined by male doct by type of area

	Total		Non-London metropolitan		County		London Borough	
	No.	%	No.	%	No.	%	No.	
Refer to female partner	143	53	67	59	28	50	48	
Refer to practice nurse	55	20	12	11	14	25	29	
Transfer to hospital/clinic	20	7	7	6	2	4	11	
Transfer to other practice	15	6	2	2	3	5	10	
Accept refusal	7	3	2	2	1	2	4	
Female chaperone	5	2	1	1	1	2	3	
Persuasion	4	1	1	1	2	4	1	
Total respondents answering question (base for %)	272		113		56		103	

Our results show that women may indeed face difficulties in obtaining an examination by a woman doctor. Ahmad et al (1989) found that while 62% of Pakistani women, 21% of Indian women and 23% of Caucasian women would object to examination by a male doctor, nonetheless linguistic and cultural concordance took precedence over gender in the choice of doctor. He hypothesised that women often did not consult their GPs for gynaecological conditions. The extent to which problems arise over examination is examined further below, and in the interviews.

4.4 ASSESSMENT, EXAMINATION AND TREATMENT

In a set of three open questions, respondents were asked whether any specific issues arose in assessment, examination or treatment of elderly patients from black or ethnic minorities, apart from communication problems.

4.4.1 Assessment

With regard to assessment, 171 GP respondents (66%) said no specific issues arose in relation to elderly black and minority ethnic patients. This response varied between types of area, from 73% in the London Boroughs to 67% in the counties and 59% in the non-London metropolitan areas. These results suggest that the higher the proportion of 'minority' patients, the less likely GPs are to perceive any specific difficulties in assessment. The differences between types of area may be partly explained by the difference in response by ethnic origin of respondent. Asian respondents were more likely to think that there were no differences than those of white UK origin (73% and 56% respectively).

Where differences were perceived, there was little consensus on what they were: a wide range was reported, including differences in patient perceptions and interpretation (23 respondents), linguistic problems (16), poor medical histories (13), vague multiple symptoms and somatism (9), and particular difficulty in assessing mental health (7).

4.4.2 Examination

One hundred and eighty-three GP respondents (70%) said no specific issues arose in examination, and again this varied by type of area from 77% in the London Boroughs to 73% in the counties and 65% in the non-London metropolitan areas. Some of the variation in response may be explained by the ethnic origin of the GP respondent: 63% of white UK respondents compared with 71% of Asian respondents saw no differences.

Table 4k: Action taken by GP respondent on refusal by elderly woman to be examined by male doctor, for white UK and Asian GP respondents

	White UK		Asian	
	No.	%	No.	%
Refer to female partner	91	64	38	38
Refer to practice nurse	23	16	25	25
Transfer to hospital/clinic	3	2	16	16
Transfer to other practice	10	7	4	4
Accept refusal	2	1	5	5
Female chaperone	2	1	2	2
Persuasion	2	1	1	1
Other	2	1	2	2
Not applicable/Don't know	9	6	13	13
Female respondent	12	8	5	5
Total respondents (base for %)	142		100	

By far the most commonly reported difficulty was female modesty, which was mentioned by 19% in the London Boroughs, 17% in non-London metropolitan areas and 10% in the counties. This reflects the findings on availability of women doctors reported above; in the London Boroughs, where access to female GPs appears more difficult, respondents were most likely to mention the issue of female modesty.

4.4.3 Treatment

With regard to treatment of elderly people from black and minority ethnic groups, 163 GP respondents (63%) felt there were no specific issues – a rather lower proportion than with assessment or examination. The proportion again varied by type of area, from 57% in non-London metropolitan areas to 71% in the counties and 65% in the London Boroughs. Also as with assessment and examination, differences in response were related to the ethnic origin of the respondent: 70% of Asian respondents saw no specific difficulties compared with 53% of white UK respondents.

The biggest single issue reported was compliance, which was mentioned by 34 GP respondents (13%). Other problems reported were high demand for medication (16), misunderstanding of instructions (15), dietary and religious laws (8) and high expectations of success (5).

Problems of compliance were widely reported in the interviews, and are described in greater detail in Chapter 6.

Taking the responses for assessment, examination and treatment together, it is possible to identify a somewhat different perception of elderly black and minority ethnic patients between GP respondents who were themselves from minority ethnic groups and those who were not. Black and minority ethnic elderly patients with white UK GPs are more likely to be seen as presenting specific problems or differences in assessment, examination and treatment. This is clearly an important finding with implications for GP training. A training need in these issues was self-identified by respondents, as the results on a question on possible further training show (see 4.11.2).

4.5 HEALTH CHECKS FOR OVER-75s

The newly-introduced obligation on GPs to offer health checks to over-75s provided an excellent opportunity to ask more focussed questions about services for elderly black or minority ethnic populations. Since these covered some of the same areas as the previous questions on assessment and examination, they provided a check on previous answers.

A multiple-choice question about any specific problems that arose in providing or carrying out health checks amongst any groups of black or minority ethnic over-75s was asked. Table 41 shows the results. While the majority of GP respondents reported no specific problems, each suggested problem area elicited a positive response from a significant minority. It was noticeable that this question elicited greater reporting of problems than the previous open-ended question on difficulties with assessment. The difference in reporting may have been due to the format of the question; or perhaps the formal obligation to provide over-75s' health checks had compelled GP respondents to approach them more systematically, and had heightened awareness of the needs.

e 41: Specific problems in over-75s' health checks among elderly black or minority ethnic groups, /pe of area

	Total		Non-London metropolitan		County		London Borough	
	No.	%	No.	%	No.	%	No.	%
ɔroblems	158	59	65	59	28	54	65	61
ᵼmunication during								
ᵼks	66	25	24	22	17	33	25	24
uptake	52	19	22	20	9	17	21	20
ᵼal health assessment	43	16	14	13	11	21	18	17
ᵼcising service	32	12	12	11	8	15	12	11
ical examination	30	11	14	13	7	13	9	8
ᵼl support assessment	29	11	6	5	8	15	15	14
·ing/sight assessment	24	9	6	5	5	10	13	12
ᵼ respondents								
ᵼ for %)	268		110		52		106	

Percentages add up to more than 100 since some respondents reported more than one problem

Overall 41% of GP respondents thought that providing or carrying out health checks on over-75s among some black or minority ethnic groups presented specific challenges. Slightly more white UK than Asian respondents mentioned particular needs to be addressed (44% and 34% respectively). Communication was the biggest single issue reported, and not surprisingly was mentioned by a slightly higher proportion of white UK than Asian respondents. Respondents in the counties were most likely to report problems, and these lay mainly in communication; as was noted earlier, fewer interpreting facilities were available in the counties.

These results suggest that it would be valuable to carry out a monitoring exercise on over 75s' health checks among black and minority ethnic patients and to ensure that primary health carers have adequate resources to do them.

4.6 SPECIFIC HEALTH NEEDS OR PROBLEMS

The questionnaire asked GP respondents whether any of their elderly black or minority ethnic patient groups had specific health needs or problems. The research interests of the medical profession have tended to concentrate on diseases and drug reactions specific to particular black and minority ethnic groups, although more recently there has been an increasing focus on the high incidence in such groups of the common preventable diseases prevalent in Western society. To what extent are such pre-occupations reflected in the interests and awareness of general practitioners?

There was marked variation by area in response to a Yes/No question, with 37% in the London Boroughs, 27% in the non-London metropolitan areas and 18% in the counties saying that groups of their elderly black or minority patients had specific health problems. Thus although GP respondents in the areas with the highest numbers of these patients were least likely to perceive them as presenting special difficulty, they were most likely to see them as having specific needs or problems.

No stereotyped approach to the definition of 'specific needs or problems' emerged. Certain individual patients, or small black or minority ethnic groups, were seen as having key problems. These lay either in special and documented risk of certain diseases, or in the particular socio-economic or environmental nature of the local area, or other problems based on the respondent's subjective experience.

The biggest single specific problem identified was diabetes (20 respondents). Other categories were the need for health education (16), the need for social support (15), hypertension (14), loneliness and isolation (12). Topics mentioned by only one or two respondents were environmental stress, depression, general health and the need for more consultation time. Language and communication were not mentioned. Responses did not vary much by ethnic origin of respondent except for the need for health education. Of the 16 respondents who mentioned this, 15 were of black or minority ethnic origin.

In view of the body of research which now exists, it is surprising that in the sample as a whole there was so little mention of specific health risks in areas such as diabetes, hypertension and coronary heart disease.

It is also worth noting that although many references to the importance of addressing the 'specific needs' of black and ethnic minorities can be found in the literature on good practice, only 27% of GP respondents perceived them to exist and there was little consensus on what they comprised. A similar picture emerged from interviews with other members of primary health care teams. These issues are further discussed below.

These findings are consistent with those from the other questions about specific needs in terms of assessment, examination, treatment and health checks. It appears that the majority of GPs who care for black or minority ethnic elderly people do not perceive them as having specific needs within primary health care, although numbers were generally higher for Asian than white UK respondents on this. On the other hand, a wide range of specific issues which can arise in the care of such patients were highlighted by small numbers of respondents.

4.7 LIAISON WITH OTHER SERVICE PROVIDERS

Multi-professional and inter-agency collaboration, liaison, or 'networking' has been widely recognised as a fundamental principle of good practice in service provision to elderly people in general, and particularly to sub-groups such as those from black and ethnic minorities who may require special consideration. The extent of inter-agency liaison at the FHSA level was assessed in Section 2. To what extent did the general practitioners in this sample work with other service providers involved in the care of these groups of patients?

In a multiple-choice question respondents were asked about the extent of their contact with the local District Health Authority, Social Services, FHSA or voluntary organisations in relation to elderly black or minority ethnic people. The question covered information guidelines, training and discussion of racial or cultural issues in relation to individual elderly patients; respondents were also asked to give any other topics on which they liaised. On the whole contact rates with any agency were low, as the following results show.

The number of GP respondents who reported having received *information guidelines* from any agency was 58: 25 in the non-London metropolitan areas, eight in the counties and 25 in the London Boroughs. In all types of area the agency mentioned least frequently as a provider of information guidelines was the District Health Authority.

Almost no *inter-agency training* was reported. In the London Boroughs five respondents said they had had training (given by Social Services, the voluntary sector and the FHSA); no-one in the non-London metropolitan areas reported any training, and only one in the counties, given by the voluntary sector. It is possible that more positive responses would have been obtained had the question focussed on race equality training in general, and not just on elderly people.

Higher responses might have been expected to a question on the extent of *liaison over individual cases*, partly because GP services deal mainly with individual patients, and partly because elderly people's health problems are often multi-factorial and require input from several agencies at once. Again, however, very low levels of contact were reported. The highest was from the London Boroughs, where eleven respondents (10%) said they had discussed individual cases with other agencies; seven positive responses came from the non-London metropolitan areas and five from the counties. The majority of the contacts were with Social Services.

In a further question, respondents were asked which of any *services or professionals specifically provided* for elderly black or minority ethnic patients they used most. Ninety-five respondents (34%) gave a nil response. A range of services was mentioned by the other respondents including:–

Social Services (11 respondents)

Interpreters (8)

Home Helps (5)

District Nurses (4)

Community Psychiatric Nurses (2)

Community Nurses with range of languages (2)

Meals-on-wheels (2)

Consultant domiciliary visits, DSS, Housing dept, Asian Day Centre (1)

All these results show a generally low level of liaison between GP respondents and other services in relation to elderly people from black and minority ethnic groups. They also confirm the results of other surveys which have found low levels of contact between GPs and community health and care services. Low referral rates by GPs have been suggested as one of the reasons for this lack of contact; this issue was raised in the interviews.

The GP has a central role in the referral of patients to other services. This role is potentially of particular significance in the health care of elderly black and minority ethnic people, in view of their high registration rates and high uptake of GP services. The results of this survey suggest that there is room for considerably more contact of all kinds between GPs and other agencies who could potentially be involved in the care of black and minority ethnic elderly people.

4.8 REFERRAL TO OTHER SERVICES

4.8.1 Health Authority services

GP respondents were asked whether they approached referral of elderly patients from black or minority ethnic groups to health authority services differently from referral of indigenous elderly patients. Only 14 (5%) said they did: four would indicate if a translator or interpreter was needed, three would try to refer to a consultant from a minority ethnic background and two would request that the patient take an interpreter with him/her. Other answers included writing a much more detailed referral letter, particularly in the case of mental health problems, involving a specialist social worker, doing more routine interpreting over the telephone for the consultant themselves, or arranging the appointment themselves. Each of these was mentioned once only. Such answers indicate an awareness of the practical problems facing the patient rather than any perception of 'difference' in either health need or service need. It is surprising that so few respondents reported arrangements of this nature. It may be that they were seen as trivial, and therefore not worth reporting.

Referral was further explored in the interviews; the evidence reinforces the conclusion that referral practice is barely modified where elderly patients from black and minority ethnic groups are concerned. It also shows that where GP respondents reported contact with other agencies in relation to these patients, it consisted mainly of discussions with consultants about the linguistic and cultural needs of patients to be admitted to hospital.

4.8.2 Social Services
The same question was asked with reference to Social Services. As with referral to health services, only a tiny minority of GP respondents (15, 5%) said they approached referral any differently, and no single pattern in the responses emerged. Answers included: involving a worker from the community, going to a specific social worker or care manager, requesting interpreting help, giving more detail in referral letters and requesting specific diets.

One respondent said that he did not approach referral differently and that as a result such patients were ultimately "deprived of amenities at home". Another commented that the Social Services in his area were poor generally, and a third said that the need for referrals for meals on wheels and home helps was less amongst this group of patients.

4.9 KNOWLEDGE OF SPECIFIC SERVICES
The extent to which referrals to specific services are made is obviously related to knowledge of any specific services. One of the aims of the survey was to assess the level of GP awareness on any specific local services for black or minority ethnic elderly people. Respondents were asked to record which of a range of possible services they thought were provided in their area.

It was stressed that respondents were not being asked to collect or collate precise information, but only to record what they already knew. Respondents with high numbers of black or minority ethnic elderly patients were expected to be more aware of the services available, while those with smaller numbers were thought unlikely to have collected, or been provided with, comprehensive information on services for these groups.

The results were matched up with the results of the parallel survey of provision for these groups by District Health Authorities and Social Service Departments (see Chapter 1). Matched data were available for ten of the fifteen FHSA areas from which the GP sample was drawn. GP respondents were not asked about provision in relation to a specific health or local authority, but only to record what was available 'in their area'. The lack of a precise definition may account for some of the discrepancy in the results of GP and health or local authority reports.

4.9.1   Health Authority services
Interpreting services
In only four of the ten FHSA areas did the services reported by the majority of GP respondents match those reported by DHAs. In the other six areas many GPs were either unaware of services reported by their DHA, or thought that services were available which had not been recorded by the DHA.

Community nursing services
An extremely confused picture emerged, with wide discrepancies between what the GPs reported and the DHAs claimed. In four areas at least half the GPs thought that specific community nurses were available, while their DHAs did not report this. There was total agreement on service provision in only two areas.

It is probable that in areas where an interpreting or linkworking service was available to community nurses, this was recorded by GPs as a specific community nursing service. In fact such facilities are generally located in maternity and child health services, and few are available specifically to those working with elderly people. It is also likely that nursing staff from black or minority ethnic backgrounds were perceived by some GPs as 'specific' to certain communities, although there was no evidence from the DHAs that they had been employed on this basis.

Mental health services (acute and community)
Results matched for four areas only. In some areas where the DHA said that a specific service was provided, only a minority of the GP respondents were aware of it. In two areas GPs claimed specific services which were not reported by the DHA.

In-patient catering
Again a picture of very incomplete knowledge emerged. A minority of GP respondents in all areas for which there was matched data thought that their

HA provided specific meals. One of these areas provided vegetarian food only, and the others bought in meals. There was complete concordance in one area where both DHA and all GP respondents reported that nothing specific was provided.

Personal needs of in-patients
On the whole DHAs reported little provision for specific personal needs, and GP respondents were generally aware of this. A small minority of GPs in seven of the areas reported that women doctors were available on request, while this was not reported by their DHAs. In one area where the DHA said that it provided some individual rooms and showers for patients from minority ethnic groups, only one GP respondent was aware of this.

4.9.2   Social Services
Interpreting services
In six of the ten areas for which matched data were available, GP respondents said that Social Services provided interpreting services, although the departments recorded only that they provided lists of interpreters available within the area. In two areas where the departments said they provided interpreting services, only a minority of GP respondents appeared to be aware of this.

Meals-on-wheels
Eight of the Social Service Departments said they provided specific meals-on-wheels, but this was reported by only three GP respondents out of the total sample.

Home help
Six of the local authorities said that a specific service was available, but this was recorded by only one GP respondent out of the total sample.

Day centres/lunch clubs
Seven of the local authorities reported specific day centres or lunch clubs in their area. Only four GP respondents in the total sample, however, reported that they were available locally.

Residential care
Three of the Social Service Departments said that some specific residential care was available, but this was recorded by only three GP respondents in total. One GP mistakenly thought it was available locally.

The discrepancies in the information provided by the different sources are so great and so widespread that they are unlikely to be due simply to differences in definition, and suggest that many GPs do not have a clear picture of what is provided in their areas, or who provides services. Other studies have suggested that GPs are generally not a good source of information on services, in spite of being well-placed to distribute appropriate information to clients in need, particularly where elderly people are concerned (Roberts et al, 1991). The results reported here suggest that the flow of information to GPs on local service availability in relation to black and minority ethnic communities should be improved. GPs are in a poor position to make appropriate referrals, or contribute to service planning and development, if their knowledge of what is – or is not – available is sketchy or misconceived.

It may be that distribution of local service information is regarded as a task more appropriately undertaken by other members of primary health care teams than by GPs. It should be noted, however, in making any recommendations, that amongst this particular sample there was a high number of single-handed GPs and small practices, and that there were generally low levels of access to practice nurses.

4.10 ATTITUDES AND PERCEPTIONS

Some more general open questions were asked to gain insight into GP perceptions of elderly people from black or minority ethnic groups.

4.10.1 Reasons for high GP consultation rates

Respondents were reminded that research has shown high general practice consulting rates by the elderly people from black or minority ethnic groups, and asked how they would account for this.

These results were not broken down by area because of the generally small numbers in each category. One striking area difference, however, did emerge: more than twice as many GP respondents in the London Boroughs as in the other areas denied high consulting rates.

Table 4m: GP respondents' explanations for high consultation rates

	No.	%
Not true in my experience	57	24
Different health beliefs/expectations	47	20
Return visits	39	16
Isolation/loneliness	25	10
Trivial worries	22	9
Mental health problems	17	7
Poor physical health	13	5
Free health service	6	3
Can't compare/no opinion	37	15
Total respondents answering question (base for %)	239	

NB: Percentage adds up to more than 100 because some GPs gave more than one reason

An interesting feature of the responses as a whole is the preponderance of non-medical or non-clinical reasons suggested for high consulting rates. The emphasis is either on different health behaviour or on the language barriers to understanding or complying with treatment. Poorer physical health was mentioned by only 13 (5% of total responses), of whom only one respondent was of Asian origin. Mental health problems were mentioned by only 23 (10% of responses). It will be seen, however, that the difficulty of diagnosing and treating mental health problems received much more comment in the interviews.

The low priority accorded to health problems seems at variance with data on the health experience of elderly people from black and minority ethnic groups. As noted earlier, both national and local morbidity and mortality data have shown a high morbidity in common preventable diseases such as diabetes, coronary heart disease and strokes. Other studies have shown high rates of consultation for non-trivial illnesses in this group (Balarajan et al, 1989; Gillam et al, 1989; Blakemore, 1982; Johnson et al, 1983).

Various explanations for this discrepancy are possible. It may be that GP respondents' perceptions of consultations with some elderly black or minority ethnic patients are dominated by difficulties in the non-medical aspects, such as communication. It is also possible that what some respondents perceive as differences in health belief or behaviour mask a real difficulty for the patient in getting a full and thorough diagnosis or explanation: for some respondents, stereotyped perceptions of such patients as 'different', or 'over-anxious', or 'demanding' may divert attention from the patient's actual health experience.

It is clear from the explanations offered for high consultation rates that many GP respondents perceive some elderly patients from black or minority ethnic groups as having specific difficulties, though largely non-medical in nature. Return visits were offered as an explanation by 16%; suggested reasons included misunderstanding of treatments and medication instructions, poor diagnosis, and misunderstanding and anxiety about condition. It is evident that poor communication between doctor and patient and a lack of appropriate written materials are still major sources of difficulty, despite attention to these aspects of health service development in recent years. Such return visits are a sad waste of both doctor's and patient's time. The unsatisfactory nature of many consultations within primary health care is further explored in the interviews.

The most common explanation offered for high consultation rates was differences in expectations of health care and medicine, or in perceptions of the role of the doctor. If this does indeed result in a significant number of extra visits, then it may be more of a problem for the doctor than for the patient. Increased availability of health education or counselling and other advice services may be able to meet some of the need now being expressed through visits to the GP.

Stresses arising through family relationships and living arrangements were another possible explanation offered; these are described more fully in the report of the interview study. Such problems are more appropriately dealt with by day and respite care facilities, housing improvements and so on than by medical intervention. This is discussed further in Chapter 6.

4.10.2 The role of primary health carers in the provision of appropriate services

Respondents were also asked the most important ways in which they could contribute to the provision of appropriate health care services for elderly patients from black or minority ethnic communities. Like the last, this question elicited a wide range of answers.

The majority of responses fell into two categories, each being mentioned by approximately one-third of the GPs answering this question. One concerned the GP's attitude to the patient: factors relating to improvements in the doctor-patient relationship – increased understanding of cultures, more time, patience or sympathy for the patient. The other major group of responses related to the provision of specific facilities – specific staff, services, clinics, women doctors, interpreters.

While the overall patterns of responses between white UK and Asian respondents were similar, there were some notable differences in emphasis. Respondents of Asian origin were significantly more likely to mention a need for specific facilities than white UK respondents (χ^2 = 4.1, DF[1], p < .05), and slightly less likely to emphasise the need for changes in GP attitudes. Among the factors which appeared less often, more Asian than white UK respondents mentioned the need for more information and encouragement to use services, and the need for extra health education. White UK respondents were more likely to mention a role for needs identification and audit exercises or, conversely, to say all patients should be treated alike.

Although respondents of Asian origin were more likely to highlight the needs for specific services, neither group of respondents saw much need for a strategic role for GPs in local service planning in relation to services for groups such as black or minority ethnic communities. There was very little emphasis on area profiles or local health needs assessment. General race equality policy was barely mentioned. This pattern was echoed in the interviews.

e 4n: Respondents' views on the most important ways in which GPs can contribute to the provision of
opriate health care services for their elderly black or minority ethnic patients; for white UK and Asian
respondents

	White UK		Asian	
	No.	%	No.	%
nges in GP attitudes	39	38	27	33
nic monitoring/Equal opportunities	4	4	3	4
e specific facilities	26	25	32	40
re community liaison	5	5	2	2
re info/encouragement to use services	5	5	16	20
differences/treat same	19	19	10	12
re health education	5	5	7	9
tification/audit of needs	9	9	–	–
er	11	11	7	9
applicable	9	9	3	4
't know	6	6	7	9
l respondents answering question (base for %)	102		81	

Percentages add to more than 100 because some GPs gave more than one response

4.10.3 Reasons for low uptake of community health services

Respondents were reminded that research has consistently shown low uptake
of community health and social care services by elderly people from black
and minority ethnic groups, and asked to comment on the reasons for this.
Only nine respondents denied that uptake is low.

As with the other attitudinal questions reported above, while the overall
response patterns for white UK and Asian respondents was similar, there were
striking diffrences in the priority attached to different factors. The proportion of Asian respondents mentioning family support was less than half that
of white UK respondents. This difference is highly significant ($\chi^2 = 6.56$,
DF^1, $p < .01$). Asian respondents were more likely to mention lack of client
awareness and knowledge of services, and problems due to language barriers.
They were twice as likely to mention poor responsiveness and inflexibility in
the services themselves as barriers, as well as lack of health education, low
expectations and pride amongst patients.

These are interesting differences, although caution is needed because the
numbers are small. That the existence of family support explains low service
uptake amongst black or minority ethnic elderly people has been widely
condemned as a 'myth' by many commentators, particularly those from the
black or minority ethnic communities themselves. In the face of the difficulties faced by such clients in gaining access to support and services, the
question of the extent to which family support actually reduces or suppresses
the potential demand for service support remains unresolved.

Table 4o: Respondents' explanations for low uptake of community health and social care services, for white UK and Asian GP respondents

	White UK		Asian	
	No.	%	No.	%
Existence of family support	38	34	17	18
Lack of knowledge of services	28	25	32	34
Language barriers	25	22	26	38
Culturally inappropriate services	11	10	8	9
Poor confidence in mainstream	11	10	9	10
Poor response/inflexibility of services	8	7	14	15
Lack of health education/low expectation	4	4	11	12
Pride	2	2	8	9
Travel problems	1	1	2	2
Respondent disagrees	5	4	3	3
Don't know	12	11	10	11
Other	11	10	6	6
Not applicable	4	4	1	1
Total respondents answering question (base for %)	112		94	

NB: Percentages add to more than 100 because some GPs gave more than one response

These issues were raised by many of the interviewees, and are explored in greater depth in the analysis of interview data. Much of the material bears witness more to the sensitivity and complexity of the issues surrounding family care amongst black or minority ethnic communities than to any community self-sufficiency.

No respondents mentioned one of the main reasons for low uptake demonstrated by a recent study – namely the lack of referrals of this client group to community health services by GPs themselves (Badger et al, 1989). These results suggest that this is a particular blind spot, to which the attention of the profession should be drawn. Any potential extra demands made of Asian GPs in referring non-English speaking elderly patients should be specifically addressed. This would be a first key step in developing primary health care as a source for referral to other services. The lack of referrals by GPs was raised in interviews, and is further discussed later.

It is disturbing that factors such as linguistic difficulties and lack of knowledge of services are still identified as important barriers to service access; these problems were identified at least a decade ago and the provision of interpreting facilities and the translation of leaflets, posters etc. have featured highly in good practice initiatives. This suggests a continuing need for educational programmes to tackle attitudes and ignorance in both clients and service providers. This does not mean, of course, that attitudes amongst general practitioners have not changed considerably; no data are available with which to compare the results of this particular study.

4.11 EDUCATION AND TRAINING

The results reported in Section 4.7 suggest that GP respondents had received very little post-vocational training in racial or cultural issues from other agencies. A further question was asked on whether respondents had received any education or training at any stage in their medical education on the particular needs of elderly people from black and minority ethnic groups. Because of the need to keep the questionnaire as short as possible, no specific details were sought.

4.11.1 Extent of training

Two hundred and thirteen (82%) of the GP respondents said they had received none. Of those who reported having had training, twelve said they had received it as undergraduates, twelve during vocational training, and twenty post-vocational. Nine respondents said they had been educated in other ways, including visits to relevant countries or by being members of minority ethnic communities themselves. Three said it was unnecessary or that they were not interested.

If these results are combined with the answers to the question about training by external agencies, it appears that currently the single biggest source of training on racial and cultural issues is post-graduate medical training. To the extent that local population composition is highly relevant to such training, this may be appropriate. More general training in race equality issues is of benefit, however, to all those working in the health services. Ideally this should be given earlier, but post-vocational training programmes are likely to be necessary for some time, particularly as those who qualified more than a decade ago would have been unlikely to have received any such training.

4.11.2 Topics for further training

Respondents were also asked what topics would be most useful in any further training on the particular needs of elderly people from black and minority ethnic groups. A clear preference emerged amongst the 134 respondents who gave details.

These responses reveal a predominating interest in the immediate issues affecting individual patient behaviour and need, rather than in the more general topics such as local demography, morbidity or service planning requirements. However a host of other topics was mentioned which included information on any specific local services, community care, community

Table 4p: Topics suggested for further training; those making any suggestion

	No.	%
Religious/cultural traditions	43	32
Mental health/psychology	13	10
Specific health risks	13	10
Health beliefs/perceptions	11	8
GPs to learn languages	4	3
Further training unnecessary	29	21
Other	33	24
Don't know	16	12
Total respondents answering question (base for %)	135	

Table 4q: Respondents' views on format for further training

	No.	%
Lectures at postgraduate centre/local hospital	120	56
Resourced discussions within GP groups	62	29
Short block GP courses	47	22
Multi-professional groups with other agencies	80	38
On a practice team basis	47	22
Audio-visual packs	63	30
Documentary material	40	19
Other	10	5
Not applicable	15	7
Total respondents answering question (base for %)	213	

NB: Percentage adds to more than 100 because most respondents gave two or more answers

development approaches, transcultural gerontology, multi-disciplinary working, integration, local issues and demography. It is clear that some respondents were highly aware of the training needed if a high quality of care is to be given to this patient group, although such awareness was not widespread. The extent to which such interest and awareness could be used and developed needs further exploration.

Respondents were asked a multiple-choice question on how they thought any further training on the particular needs of elderly people from black and minority ethnic groups could best be given. More respondents expressed preferences on mode of training, than on actual topic. Table 4q sets out the results.

Sessions at the local post-graduate medical centre were the most frequently selected format, chosen by 120 (56%) of the GP respondents. Multi-disciplinary groups was selected by 80 (38%), audio-visual packs by 63 (30%) and resourced discussions within GP groups by 62 (29%).

4.12 SUMMARY OF FINDINGS

The findings can be most usefully discussed in conjunction with those from the interview study, since the latter furthered our understanding of some responses about which we could only conjecture in the postal survey. However, the main findings can be briefly summarised. While respondents of Asian origin demonstrated much greater insight into the particular needs of their elderly patients from black and minority ethnic groups than those of White UK origin, this difference had limited impact on service delivery. In general, there is little to indicate a specific approach to any elderly patients from black and minority ethnic groups: very few GP respondents recorded the ethnic origin of their patients; they had little access to formal interpreting services (despite the fact that only a quarter of the GPs reported having no communication problems); apart from the recognition that particular issues arose due to differences in language, culture and knowledge there was little awareness of any differences in health care need between the elderly indigenous population and those from black or minority ethnic groups; few GPs thought there were specific issues to be addressed in providing care for any of these groups; there was little liaison about them with other agencies; limited knowledge of other agencies' services for them; and very little prior training concerning their care.

5 INTERVIEW STUDY OF MEMBERS OF PRIMARY HEALTH CARE TEAMS: RESEARCH METHODS AND CHARACTERISTICS OF THE SAMPLE

5.1 AIMS OF THE STUDY

The interview study had two main aims. One was to gain more comprehensive data on primary health care for elderly people from black and minority ethnic groups, by supplementing the information gained from GPs in the postal survey with information from other members of primary health care teams; this would allow some comparison of the answers given by different professional groups. The other was to explore some of the key problems or areas of need in greater depth, both with GPs and with the other health professionals.

Individual in-depth interviews were carried out with 41 professionals working in primary health care, and a group interview was held with Linkworkers in one area. General Practitioners, Practice Nurses, Linkworkers and Health Liaison Officers, Community Nurses, specialist FHSA staff and a Practice Manager were included in the interview sample.

5.2 SELECTION OF THE SAMPLE

Interviews were carried out in six areas, selected to represent as well as possible the sample of FHSA areas included in the GP postal survey. Two FHSA areas were selected from each of the three FHSA sampling bands used in the GP postal survey (see Section 3.2). The six areas were chosen to reflect a balance of (a) geographical characteristics, and (b) degree of FHSA interest in the health care needs of black and minority ethnic communities. This was assessed on the basis of the results of the postal survey of FHSAs, interviews with FHSA staff and published reports.

A random sample of general practitioners was selected from those who had responded to the GP postal survey in each of the six selected FHSA areas, in which key characteristics such as gender, ethnic origin and size of practices of respondents were balanced as far as possible.

The original intention had been to carry out approximately seven interviews in each area consisting of (a) three GPs, (b) one Linkworker, and (c) three nurses chosen from the same practices as the GPs. However, it transpired that very few of the selected practices employed or had attached Linkworkers, Practice Nurses, or other Community Nurses, who were also willing or available to be interviewed at the time of the study. Unfortunately because of constraints of time, part of the study was carried out during the holiday months of August and September.

Interviewees were therefore identified from a variety of sources – some were working in the practices of other GP postal survey respondents in the same vicinity as those selected for the interview study, and some were known by various local services to be working in areas with a high proportion of black and minority ethnic residents.

The final sample consisted of 18 GPs, six Practice Nurses, seven Linkworker or health liaison officers, nine Community Nurses, and one practice manager.

5.3 RESEARCH METHODS

A semi-structured interview schedule was used (see Appendix C), with a set of core questions which was asked of each of the professional groups. Nurses and Linkworkers were also asked some of the questions from the GP postal survey questionnaire, including ethnic origin record-keeping, communication, consultation procedures, specific needs, inter-agency liaison and training.

Each professional group was asked a few further questions appropriate to their specific role within primary health care, on some of the more sensitive issues including the needs of individual and family carers, relationships between Linkworkers (or other community liaison workers) and other primary health care team members, and general levels of care within local communities. Two further content areas included the general role of Linkworkers and other health liaison workers in primary health care, about which very little is known, and the use and evaluation of health education materials with these particular groups.

The results of the study were grouped by profession and each group was analysed separately. The reason for this was to uncover any inter-professional variation in approach to elderly patients from black or minority ethnic groups. Any trends detected, of course, must be considered with caution in the absence of substantiation amongst much bigger samples. There is no reason to suspect, however, that the sample of professionals interviewed is particularly unrepresentative in any way, with the one exception that they all worked in areas with significant black or minority ethnic populations.

For the purposes of analysis the results were divided into Community Nurses; Practice Nurses; Linkworkers, Advocates and Health Liaison Officers; and General Practitioners.

5.4 CHARACTERISTICS OF THE SAMPLE

5.4.1 Community nurses (9)

The sample consisted of health visitors and district nurses. One district nurse and one health visitor were at the time of the study in management positions. The Community Nurses were mainly aged between 46–55 years. One was

Chinese, one Afro-Caribbean and the others were white British. Four were employed by practices, one by the FHSA, and the rest by DHAs. All were female.

5.4.2 Practice nurses (6)

The Practice Nurses were aged from 25 to 66 years. One had recently returned from retirement to work a few hours per week, partly to help with the over-75s health checks. Five of the Practice Nurses were white British, one was Asian, and one was of mixed origin. Hours varied from six hours per week to full-time. All were female.

5.4.3 Linkworkers (7)

Because the role of the Linkworker in primary health care is less familiar, and more developmental than the others, the sample is described in greater detail. The term 'Linkworker' is used throughout for convenience, although the actual job titles included Asian Liaison Health Worker, Asian Health Worker, Health Linkworker, and Health Advocate.

Services such as linkworking, health liaison, interpreting and advocacy are provided in a variety of ways, and are used within different contexts. The criteria used in the selection of the interviewees were (a) employment by a DHA or FHSA, (b) providing services mainly to community and primary health care workers, (c) having elderly clients, and (d) not employed solely as interpreters.

In several areas there appeared to be only one employee who met these criteria and fortunately each of them agreed to be interviewed. Interviewees in two areas turned out to have limited contact with patients in the general practice setting. These findings tend to confirm GP comments in the postal survey about the limited availability of such services in their areas.

The Linkworkers in the sample were employed by their DHA or FHSA; four were joint appointments, one between the DHA and the Local Authority. Only three had full-time appointments. Their line management was located in different departments – community health, the local community centre, the FHSA, the Health Promotion Unit; two of those with joint appointments had two line managers, whose interests they had to balance. Four were Asian, one Somali, one Chinese and one was Turkish. Six were female, and one male. Their ages ranged from 25 to 55 years.

The number of patients seen varied considerably between Linkworkers. All except two employed within specific services worked with a wide range of health and other welfare staff.

One of the aims of the interview study was to identify the scope of the role of the Linkworkers in the provision of primary and community health care to black and minority ethnic communities. Their job descriptions were wide. All provided interpreting services, and most had additional remits in promoting awareness amongst professionals, disseminating information to clients in both oral and written forms, and community liaison. Some also had responsibilities in a varied combination of health education and promotion, client advocacy, translating and needs identification within the community. Many of the comments below bear witness to the breadth of the Linkworker's role.

5.4.4 General practitioners (18)

Eighteen GPs were interviewed, of whom four were women. Half were aged 45 or under, and half were between 45–65 years. The ethnic composition of the sample was ten white British, six Asian, one Chinese and one Sri Lankan. Two were single-handed, five were in two-partner practices, six were in three to four-partner practices, one was in a five-partner practice and four were in six to seven-partner practices. Seven were based in health centres.

6 INTERVIEW STUDY OF MEMBERS OF PRIMARY HEALTH CARE TEAMS: THE FINDINGS

6.1 ACCESS

The need for more open, flexible access to services for some black or minority ethnic communities has been often repeated. Nurses and Linkworkers were all asked how patients were referred to them.

All except two of the nine *Community Nurses* said that they had wide referral sources within their communities. Patient contacts came through a range of statutory and community sources, and were also self-referred, as the following description illustrates:

> *"As far as I can I collect referrals from wards, from GPs and Health Visitors. I try to assess where appropriate or give advice over the phone. I can have self referrals from patients or carers. I liaise with day hospitals, accident and emergency units, and I visit homes where necessary."*

Patients reached the *Practice Nurses* through much narrower channels. They were referred only by the GPs with whom the nurses worked, or referred themselves by turning up at the surgeries and clinics. A significant source of first contacts between Practice Nurse and patients was the invitation to the over-75s health checks. As would be expected, the Practice Nurses were in contact with a much narrower section of the community.

Patients were referred to *Linkworkers* from a wide range of formal and informal sources. Local minority ethnic community centres were a focal point: referrals also came from the local hospital, day centre, community health services, health centres and clinics, particularly those where the Linkworkers were based. Many patients referred themselves, dropping in at the Linkworker's office, through informal contacts in the community, and telephoning.

> *"I visit the hospital, the day centres. I call in at the Community Centre. I see health professionals at meetings and tell them who and where I am. I meet patients at the health centre. People stop me in the streets, they come to my place in the middle of the night . . ."*

Clearly potential clients have very open access to linkworking services, where they exist.

There appeared to be strong similarities in the ways in which Linkworkers and Community Nurses operated – both had a brief to work widely within the community, to respond to local need; both had a range of contacts with many different services and were in theory fairly accessible to patients. Both were playing a role in health education and promotion within the community. To what extent did such similarities mean that they developed similar ways of working with patients such as elderly people from black and minority ethnic groups? This was one of the themes explored in the following sections.

6.2 RECORDING ETHNIC ORIGIN

Practice and Community Nurses and GPs were asked whether they recorded the ethnic origin of their patients.

Ethnic background of patients was recorded by five of the nine *Community Nurses*. Very different reasons were given for doing so, which included to aid nursing assessment, routine, out of interest, to provide important background information and to indicate potential language problems. Only one said it was to provide population information. One nurse did not record because she thought it was a difficult issue.

Like the Community Nurses, *Practice Nurses* varied in their approach to recording: two did record, and four did not.

Reflecting the results of the GP postal survey, the majority of *GP interviewees* did not record the ethnic origin of their patients. The main reasons appeared to be that they felt they knew the patients and their families anyway, or that they knew all the relevant languages, or that they had seen no particular reason to do it.

No consensus on the purpose of recording emerged amongst those who did record, some of whom had just begun the practice. Reasons included the need to know about cultural and ethnic background, the specific health risks amongst certain groups and the need for interpreting services. Only two said they recorded to build up a population profile.

It appears then that throughout the primary health care team the practice of recording ethnic origin is limited, and there is little consensus on the reasons for recording or not recording.

6.3 COMMUNICATION

6.3.1 Main methods of dealing with communication problems

The Community and Practice Nurses were asked about the frequency and nature of any communication problems between themselves and elderly patients; how they usually tackled the issue; and whether the use of family, friends or children affected the consultation in any way.

All except one of the nine *Community Nurses* had patients who did not speak English. They reported the same methods of dealing with language problems as the GPs in the postal survey, with a heavy reliance on help from families, supplemented by a little help from interpreters and Linkworkers, and sign language. Only one mentioned getting help from a colleague.

Some confidence in the use of non-verbal forms of communication such as body language was also expressed:

> *"I use body language and mime. I get over ideas, e.g. respite care . . . you'd be surprised."*

Body language is an important part of communication. Several Community Nurses referred to this. There are contexts in which verbal communication in itself has limited powers of expression, and interviewees emphasised the importance of observation of and sensitivity to body language where communication was in the hands of a third party. Some interviewees felt that where words were conveyed through interpreters, the doctor or nurse's tone, and perhaps the desire to express sympathy or understanding, could be lost. Touch might become more important in this situation.

However, the usefulness of non-verbal communication in transmitting crucial information was felt by other Community Nurses to be limited:

> *"If you have someone who is good at communicating in mime that's fair enough, but not good enough . . . amateurism can't get at the health needs of people."*

The use of family or friends as interpreters was not seen as an entirely satisfactory solution, and prompted a similar set of comments to those reported in the GP postal survey, including the loss of important information, embarrassment and inhibition over sensitive topics. The use of linkworking services is discussed below.

All except one of the six *Practice Nurses* had patients who did not speak English, and the same methods of dealing with communication problems were reported as by GPs and Community Nurses. 'Making do' clearly had a role. Like the other groups, the Practice Nurses felt that the presence of family or friends created problems of embarrassment and confidentiality in the consultation. Husbands and brothers-in-law were felt to be particularly inappropriate:

> *"Husbands are no good either. They tell their wives off. It's like World War III in here sometimes."*
> *"If it's a husband or brother sitting there, I don't know about the patient but I get embarrassed asking a man if his wife ever had a cervical smear and they say 'I've never heard of it' and I have to do drawings. I just die."*

As reported in the GP postal survey, *GP interviewees* relied heavily on family members to provide interpreting services. GPs were more inclined to worry about inaccurate translation than issues related to embarrassment and inhibition; although the constraints on consultation with family members present were widely acknowledged, it was clear that for many GPs such a system is better than nothing:

> *"Most ethnic minority elderly come with a relation – it's less confidential for the client, but better for the doctor; it affects more intimate problems."*
> *"Inevitably it affects the consultation – but I would rather have someone there who can translate, even if the quality is poor, or the translation inadequate; sometimes you take chances."*

One GP saw the problem of inhibition as not applying to elderly people:

> *"Sometimes patients are reluctant to talk in the presence of their children but the elderly have nothing to hide."*

6.3.2   Children as interpreters

All except one of the nine *Community Nurses* felt that it was totally inadequate or unfair to use children as interpreters:

> *"Professionals shouldn't put this responsibility on a child – the child's own embarrassment makes them alter things, and anyway they don't understand."*
> *"In one particular family the patient is very ill and doubly incontinent, and it's not fair on them to have to ask questions on delicate matters . . . (the child) can't say 'do you wet the bed every night? Is Mummy tired?'"*

Like the Community Nurses, the six *Practice Nurses* disliked using children as interpreters, except for one who felt that translating was a responsibility that children accepted enthusiastically and seriously. One Practice Nurse said she often refused to carry out consultations where children were brought along.

Some *GP interviewees* also felt that the superior linguistic skills of children made them useful during consultations, although others expressed doubts:

> *"Children seem to cope very well – it's fine for the doctor."*
> *"In some ways children are more sophisticated than the adults – they are more streetwise, but children don't have the experience to interpret accurately."*

Any problems which arose were seen more as problems for the patient than for the doctor:

"If it's something gynaecological it's impossible with a boy child – I say come back with a linkworker."

"They don't like children there if they are discussing personal things."

6.4 THE ROLE OF LINKWORKERS

6.4.1 Interpreting services

All interviewees were asked whether they felt that the presence of a Linkworker or interpreter affected a consultation in any way.

The relationship between *Community Nurses* and Linkworkers has been found in other studies not to be an entirely easy one (e.g. Department of Health, 1987). Quite a few of the Community Nurses' comments expressed some reservations about the presence of a third party as interpreter, although unfortunately the interviews did not always distinguish between the different kinds of interpreting services used.

"It's getting the information right and making sure the interpreter doesn't put their own interpretation on it."

"Sometimes there is no literal translation, so it has to be kept simple and this could cause problems. The effect on the patient is more difficult to assess . . . you can't easily gauge how well you get the message across. If I can get all the information over on the same level that's good. Also there's the question of how they interact . . . it might be they know each other, have a personal relationship."

One Community Nurse thought that Linkworkers needed nursing training:

"It depends on whether the Linkworker has nurse training – if so, you get teamwork, but with a Linkworker you're not always sure what's happening – you need to know them if linkworking is to be effective, a relationship has to be built."

The Community Nurse who made this comment, however, added that she was aware that this view fitted in with existing structures, where professionals like health visitors were seen to be doing their job, with Linkworkers subservient.

The *Practice Nurses* also had varying perceptions of linkworking/interpreting/advocacy services:

"All Asian patients have a lot of faith in the Linkworker, and ask for them happily. When you think of the problems there could be – I think they (the Linkworkers) have been well chosen."

"I tried using one – the standard was poor. The interpreter was answering for patients. They would interrupt, and I never felt sure that the message was getting through. Neighbours or families are better. Interpreters give a medical story, not what's bothering the patient."

GP interviewees too had mixed views. GPs who had employed their own Linkworkers or who had regular access to a Linkworker for a specific community undoubtedly valued the service:

> *"The presence of the Linkworker has a great effect – the social and the medical get mixed up if a child or a relative interprets – anecdote is presented as a physical problem – with a Linkworker it was easily sorted out."*

But clearly there were reservations about some interpreting services:

> *"I'm not sure if an independent translator is better, particularly where there are personality factors – mental illness, depression, somatisation."*
> *"Private questions are more difficult – I prefer to use my practice partner."*
> *"Like anyone, there are lots of things it's difficult to discuss with someone else there – bodily functions, gynae."*

Linkworkers were also asked what effect they thought the presence of an interpreter, linkworker or advocate had on a consultation. They said very much the same things as the other health professionals: they felt that the presence of an unknown third party could inhibit the patient from disclosing certain things, or could cause embarrassment, and that information and the expression of feelings sometimes get lost in the process of translation. One Linkworker felt unsure of the extent to which he was trusted by the health professionals. However, comments revealed that Linkworkers did nonetheless believe their presence could be helpful.

All the health professions appeared to agree on the advantages and problems of three-way consultation. However, the relationship between health professional, Linkworker and patient is clearly a delicate one. Three-way consultations appeared most likely to be perceived as successful where terms and conditions of employment enabled Linkworkers to work with other primary health carers as a team.

One observation which can be made about the findings on both family and professional interpreting, is a widely varying degree of professional tolerance of limitations imposed by communication gaps. Clearly perception of the problem, and confidence in non-verbal communication, differ and these differences affect the demand for adequate interpreting services.

Another point was made by an FHSA Ethnic Minorities Development Officer, previously a Linkworker herself: she remarked on a certain ambiguity in the attitude of some health workers, who become demanding or critical when offered formal interpreting assistance, while often welcoming and seeking out the help of family members whose linguistic skills may be poor.

It may be inferred that all staff involved in three-way consultation in primary health care need training and guidance: there needs to be a clear understanding of mutual expectations, of roles and boundaries. Some of the training resources available address these needs (e.g. training course for primary care advocates run by City & Hackney FHSA; see also guidance in London Interpreting Project, 1990; Bahl, 1987).

6.4.2 Responsibilities of the Linkworker

There is considerable evidence that Linkworkers have developed wide responsibilities within the community, and played a variety of roles including that of patient advocate. It is not clear to what extent these developments are perceived and supported by other members of the primary health care team, or to what extent Linkworkers are appreciated. For this reason the GPs and nurses were asked to whom they saw the interpreter as accountable during a consultation.

There were some conflicts of view on accountability. Linkworkers were variously seen by the *Community Nurses* as accountable to the health professional, to everyone, as a go-between, and as neutral. None mentioned the patient!

Unlike the Community Nurses, *Practice Nurses* said they thought the Linkworker was accountable to the patient.

GP interviewees gave a wide range of views on the locus of Linkworker accountability, including to themselves only, to their employers, or to the patient. Some thought the Linkworker should be neutral, or see things "from the point of view of who needs help most – it depends".

A series of questions were asked of the *Linkworkers* in order to explore their perception of their role in relation to health professional and patient, during consultations and outside them. As far as the health professional was concerned, Linkworkers saw their role as providing interpretation, acting as go-between, explaining the meaning of what the patient was saying and providing cultural awareness and information. The relationship with the patient was quite differently perceived. Linkworkers variously mentioned giving support, confidence, encouragement, health education, advice and information on wider benefits to the patient, and presenting the patient's point of view to the health professional.

The Linkworkers interviewed clearly played a very wide role in relation to the patient, and to some extent met gaps in service need, supplementing services given by professionals in primary and community health care teams. The following quotations indicate the range of the Linkworkers' responsibilities:

"Someone needed an operation, but has a problem with blood pressure, so the doctor gave him medicine but he doesn't use it properly. Every time he sees the doctor he thinks it's for the operation, but the doctors can't operate until the pressure goes down so I'm advising him about his medicine."

"If it's a case of cancer and an operation is needed, we need to support the patient to face the operation; and after the operation, if they have no family, to try to support and give positivity to life. They will think it's hopeless and that they are going to die soon and that everything is unfair to them. You can explain there is something left and suggest things . . ."

"Clients ask you about all sorts of things – you need training for everything . . . the patients need confidence, they're ashamed of not speaking the language, they're ashamed of being Asian, they don't like to ask for things, and they need a lot of encouragement. This is why the uptake of services is low. I'm pleased that the HA has allowed me to go into homes. That is the first step, and then get them to clinics."

The Linkworkers were asked whether their role as 'go-between' or any other aspect of their contacts within primary health care caused problems. Various issues were mentioned. Difficulties sometimes arose where the patient disagreed with the professional, in conveying the patient's real meaning or where misunderstandings had occurred. Patronising attitudes specifically amongst health visitors and Asian GPs were also reported. All the Linkworkers, however, said they had good or excellent relationships with health professionals; one was very enthusiastic:

"(They're) absolutely great; we love each other."

6.4.3   Skills and abilities needed by Linkworkers

All interviewees were asked what criteria they would use to judge the quality of a good interpreter within the context of primary health care.

Confidentiality, good communication skills, ability to empathise with patients, assertiveness and thoroughness were all mentioned by the *Community Nurses* as important qualities in Linkworkers. These responses show the importance attached by the Community Nurses to the Linkworkers' role in the development of a productive relationship with patients. Linguistic skills were not mentioned!

The *Practice Nurses*, on the other hand, mainly mentioned linguistic skills. *GP interviewees* also mentioned both linguistic and communication skills. Some had very high standards:

*"Linkworkers should be able to convey every nuance, be swift, and
ensure that the patient feels heard, and not get distracted."*
"Fluent, sympathetic, good communicator, warm – it's a lot!"

What qualities did the *Linkworkers* themselves emphasise? A wide range of
skills and abilities was mentioned which reflected the scope of their role.
Knowledge of medical terminology and treatment techniques and the culture, demography, health experience and literacy of the target patient group
were mentioned. Skills included counselling, communication, teaching and
training, assertion, languages and administration. Personal qualities were
sensitivity, firmness, diplomacy, and ability to respect confidentiality.

Apparently, few of the health professionals saw the Linkworkers as
interpreters only; on the contrary, great importance was placed on their
communication skills and ability to develop good relationships with patients.
One Community Nurse commented:

"Linkworkers are the best thing since sliced bread!"

Few, however, emphasised the skills mentioned by the Linkworkers in
relation to providing patient services themselves, such as welfare and other
advice, information, emotional support, counselling or health education; nor
were their skills in training or disseminating information to professionals
mentioned by the potential recipients. It appears that the scope and potential
value of the Linkworker role within the primary health care team is still
underestimated.

6.4.4 Need for additional Linkworker services

In spite of some ambiguity in their feelings about them, *Community Nurses*,
when asked, said they would like more access to interpreting services, the
main reason being to improve their communication with and understanding
of their patients.

Three of the six *Practice Nurses* also said they would like more access to such
services, of whom two said that this was so that they could attract a wider
population.

In response to a similar question, most of the *Linkworkers* thought there was a
need for more services like theirs in their area. Reasons given were the lack of
any services at the local out-patient departments and hospitals, and to carry
out more prevention and local research. In other words, while both health
professionals and Linkworkers saw the value of the Linkworker in facilitating
the services offered by the health professionals, the Linkworkers also saw
themselves as providers of patient services.

6.5 ASSESSMENT, EXAMINATION, TREATMENT, HEALTH PROMOTION, REHABILITATION AND REFERRAL

Nurse and GP interviewees were asked in detail about any issues or difficulties which arose in their work with elderly people from any black or minority ethnic group, due to cultural or linguistic differences. These questions were not included in the Linkworkers' questionnaire.

6.5.1 Reasons for consultation

Only one of the nine *Community Nurses* thought there were no differences between elderly people from different ethnic groups. The others gave a similar range of perceived differences to that of the GPs in the postal survey. These included a higher incidence of diabetes, different expectations of the consultation and more inappropriate consultations – blamed, in the latter case, on the failure of the health services to give health education and information. The responses of the *Practice Nurses* to this question were very similar.

The *GP interviewees* repeated the same range of problems as reported in the postal survey. Three focussed on consultations regarded as unnecessary:

> *"They tend to worry about a lot of small things"*
> *"They will put up with less for a shorter time"*
> *"First of all patients from ethnic minorities are very health conscious so attend for trivial reasons . . . just to satisfy them you have to do certain things, otherwise they're not satisfied and keep coming back, e.g. investigations to keep them happy."*

6.5.2 Assessment

As above, only one *Community Nurse* felt there were no differences in assessing elderly people from black and minority ethnic groups; she stressed the importance of nurses taking an 'open' approach to all patients. Most of the others commented on the difficulty of getting accurate medical histories or background information, identifying the need for the nurse to take more time, to get more detail, to be aware of any cultural factors influencing reporting and to get as much information as possible from other sources such as referral letters and medical notes, and to know the patient.

Again the responses of the *Practice Nurses* followed the same pattern. A particular emphasis was placed by one of them on her difficulty in assessing mental health:

> *"The past medical history never seems so bad as with a white person, e.g. any history of heart disease? But what do they think of as heart disease – only a heart attack? And the language barrier stops mental health assessment. I mean the way I assess, e.g. what day is it? who is the Prime Minister? – It's not valid comparing black and ethnic minority responses and those of the indigenous population."*

The majority of *GPs* in the postal survey had said there was no difference in how they approached the assessment of an elderly person from a black or minority ethnic group. However, a slightly different picture emerged from the interviews: only one said there were no differences, while six mentioned difficulties in mental health assessment (compared with seven respondents overall in the GP postal survey):

> *"In terms of mental health we get on badly, unless the patient has good English; and I think that what is normal in one culture is not necessarily so in another – I tend to let the conversation flow, and if I think there are problems perhaps I will delve. It's very individual. I will ask the family if it's possible."*

The other differences specifically mentioned echoed the main categories reported in the GP postal survey, and included different perceptions and health beliefs, and the difficulty of getting a good medical history.

6.5.3 Examination
Four of the nine *Community Nurses* reported a reluctance by some women to be examined, but all felt that with an appropriate manner they could usually overcome hesitancy. Careful explanations and a relaxed approach were mentioned. The responses of the *Practice Nurses* followed the same pattern.

The *GP interviewees* also focussed on this issue, and some felt there was not much they could do about it:

> *"There's nothing we can do if they refuse".*

6.5.4 Treatment
Compliance was certainly felt to be a problem with elderly people from black and minority ethnic groups by almost all the *Community Nurses* and *Practice Nurses*; the reasons suggested for failure to comply, however, varied enormously. Two felt that compliance was a difficulty with all elderly patients:

> *". . . (black or ethnic minority elderly people) don't always do what they are told – just like white elderly people; older people find it hard – it's to do with age, not culture."*

Four said that difficulty in comprehending or remembering treatment regimes underlay non-compliance. One believed that there was some reluctance to take responsibility for health and self-care.

Compliance was highlighted by several of the *GP interviewees*, often suggesting a possible failure to recognise or tackle underlying causes of anxiety:

> *"You can urge and encourage, but in the end it's their decision to comply or not."*

Taken together, the comments of many health professionals revealed an underlying inconsistency of attitude towards this patient group. Conflicting images were presented of a patient group which worries enough about health to make arrangements for interpretation at considerable inconvenience to closest family or friends, to make unnecessary trips to the doctor, to make high demands for medication or other treatment, and yet refuses to do the one thing which might improve health!

Some GPs had a different view:

> *"There are no problems with compliance, because the families are so careful – it's only when there are misunderstandings that compliance fails – maybe it's not connected to age or race."*

6.5.5 Health promotion/education

This was a particularly interesting area to explore with the *Community Nurses*, who are an important resource in health promotion and the prevention of ill health. Only one interviewee claimed to have significant success in health promotion with elderly Asian people: this referred principally to a project with special funding run in collaboration with an Asian nurse/Linkworker. The Linkworker was seen as a key factor in the success of the project.

Most of the other interviewees felt that this aspect of their work was less than satisfactory. It was very time-consuming, they had to compromise about what could be achieved, and it got neglected. The following quotes illustrate varying views:

> *"It will do – you can't promote health in quite the same way; you can't explain things opportunistically as they arise – it's a language difficulty because on a day-to-day basis we don't have an interpreter with us."*
>
> *"We can get it across simply – we can give advice about giving up smoking and about toileting and demonstrate and get it across."*
>
> *"Health education gets neglected: it's partly because of female modesty – there may be no one available to teach techniques of breast examination. Once someone is known and trusted, then word travels, and everyone comes."*

The *Practice Nurses* made very similar comments. *GP interviewees* did not appear to be much involved in health promotion to this patient group:

> *"Linkworkers do a great deal."*
>
> *"You really have got to employ people e.g. dieticians, interpreters and others."*
>
> *"I'm not a big leaflet man."*

One GP with many elderly black and minority ethnic patients described the challenges she faced:

"We've learned with elderly white people where to prompt and where not to try to re-educate, e.g. over bowel habits. With black and ethnic minority elderly we have to learn, and it takes twice as long, because of their language and culture."

The comments quoted in this section highlight the shortcomings in health promotion to elderly people from black and minority ethnic groups; they also hint at approaches which have been effective.

6.5.6 Rehabilitation

Five of the *Community Nurses* felt that there were specific difficulties in rehabilitation work with elderly people from black and minority ethnic groups, although different emphases emerged in the explanations for this. Patient attitudes and a lack of motivation to regain independence were mentioned by two respondents. One of the *Practice Nurses* agreed, feeling that extra encouragement was needed.

The *GP interviewees* had little involvement in rehabilitation. One felt that not much was achieved with this patient group at the local stroke clinic.

It may be conjectured that inappropriate explanation and encouragement while a patient is in hospital might lead to incomprehension and anxiety, misinterpreted as lack of motivation. Some of the Community Nurses firmly identified the source of difficulties as poor service response to need – a lack of follow-up after discharge from hospital, misunderstanding of culture within day hospital facilities and the lack of appropriate language and other skills amongst staff to educate the patient about possibilities and goals in rehabilitation, about the importance of preventive measures, and about possible health consequences.

6.5.7 Referral

Two *Community Nurses* mentioned low referral to their own services, of whom one firmly blamed GPs:

"There is a lack of referral by GPs. I ask them at least every two weeks 'Anything for me? Are you sure? I've made it my business to have good liaison with the GP. If they don't contact me, I ask them; I started monthly meetings, but this was too frequent and I ended up with meetings on my own."

The other Community Nurse felt unsure of the reasons. Three felt that the system worked well.

One *Practice Nurse* identified the lack of any counselling services to which patients could be referred:

> *"It's difficult for some patients to go into counselling – they are afraid of being labelled – will they get called schizophrenic? One of my older patients says he has been given this label because he's black – he says he's depressed – and I agree with him."*

None of the *GP interviewees* felt that there were specific problms in referral of this patient group. The major concern appeared to be the difficulty of getting referrals of all elderly people to hospital:

> *"The real problems are in waiting lists and admissions."*

6.6 OVER-75s' HEALTH CHECKS

Nurse and Linkworker interviewees were asked, as in the GP postal survey, about any specific problems in providing or carrying out over-75s' health checks among members of black or minority ethnic groups. GP and nurse interviewees were asked whether there were any differences between ethnic groups in patient response, interest or uptake, relevance or outcome. They were also asked whether any specific approaches needed to be adopted to over-75s' health checks for black or minority ethnic groups.

Conflicting views emerged amongst the *Community Nurses* on differences in uptake and relevance of over-75s' health checks. Several saw the checks as a potentially important referral route for elderly people from black or minority ethnic groups to their own services, while one said no new referrals were coming through. Two respondents said uptake was low, and two said it was high.

Some need for specific approaches was seen, either in the use of translated letters, the specific employment of a nurse from an appropriate background or through contacting patients by community networking.

It was particularly relevant to seek the views of the *Practice Nurses* on the checks. All the Practice Nurses interviewed carried them out. Little difficulty was reported: two said there were no problems, two said that publicity was the main difficulty, and one mentioned communication. In tems of assessment, mental health was mentioned once as a difficulty.

There was the same contrast in views on uptake amongst the Practice Nurses as amongst the Community Nurses. In terms of outcome, the Practice Nurses commented that they were picking up needs for diabetes treatment and for aids and adaptations.

The Practice Nurses also thought that there was a need for specific approaches to the checks with this patient group. Two of the six said it was important to go through the practice register systematically to find patients and monitor whether they had been seen. One nurse said that more interpreters and translated leaflets were needed. The Asian nurse, who did not work with Asian GPs, thought that there should be wider employment of similar staff to herself:

> *"Elderly Asian people welcome the check if it is approached in the right way and nothing is hidden. They have a fear of the unknown. You need to know who they'll take to. Many worry about going to the GP – they think the doctor won't understand – that puts a big 'no'"*

The majority of *GP interviewees* thought there was no difference in response to the checks between different ethnic groups. Views amongst those who thought there was a difference polarised around the belief either that uptake by black and minority ethnic groups was excellent, or that it was very low. Most of the GP interviewees saw no need for specific approaches. A couple said it might be important to translate letters. Like the nurses, two felt that if they had gone through the register and the GP and Practice Nurse personally contacted elderly patients or their families, there was not much else they could do.

Only two GPs reported picking up different health needs, specifying diabetes, blood pressure, weight and strokes. A more important concern was the general relevance and appropriateness of the programme:

> *"It's a waste of time."*
> *"We don't find anything we don't know about."*
> *"Whether it's worth doing is debatable – 90% of people will visit within two years, and of the 10% who don't, if you find them they're usually disgustingly healthy. That's why they don't come. They're not chained down, just healthy."*

No clear picture emerged from the interviews on the success or relevance of the checks with over-75s from black or minority ethnic groups. Perception varied by practice rather than by area. No one expressed particular enthusiasm for the importance of the checks for this patient group, or saw a particularly strong need for specific approaches.

6.7 SPECIFIC HEALTH NEEDS

Nurse interviewees were asked whether they thought there were any major differences between the health needs of any groups of black or minority ethnic elderly people and the indigenous elderly population.

Little difference was perceived by the *Community Nurses,* although two drew attention to the higher risk of diabetes, heart disease, hypertension and strokes. Differences in social need were mentioned by several, and this will be explored further below.

The views of the *Practice Nurses* were similar.

Linkworkers were asked a slightly different question: whether there were any differences between work with elderly people and other age groups. Five of the seven thought there were. Elderly people were thought to have greater language problems, to suffer greater cultural disorientation, to need considerably more health education; they demanded more patience, time and understanding. In spite of these needs, one Linkworker noted that she was not getting referrals for elderly people:

> *"Elderly people sit in a corner and don't talk. They're always concerned with the children, and they never ask about themselves. The geriatric team is their point of contact, but I have never had a reference from the district nurses or the geriatric health visitors."*

The Linkworkers clearly did think that elderly people from black or minority ethnic groups had specific needs, and that specific approaches were appropriate. The kinds of needs identified, however, did not demand a primarily clinical response; there is no simple answer to the most appropriate form of further support. Specific protocols or guidelines for procedures for over-75s health checks on such patients might prove to be a valuable approach.

6.8 USE OF HEALTH EDUCATION RESOURCES

All interviewees were asked whether they made use of any videos, translated leaflets or posters relevant to elderly black or minority ethnic patients; if they did, which they found most useful; and whether they thought more resources aimed at specific groups of elderly patients would be helpful.

Community nurses appeared to make little use of health education resources in their work with elderly people from black or minority ethnic groups. Some commented that little was available which was appropriate to elderly people, and several said that leaflets were inappropriate anyway because their elderly patients could not read:

> *"The HAs produce a lot of materials in Punjabi, and the younger patients read it. The problem is the old people from the Punjab – it's very difficult – the GPs speak Punjabi but the patients take no responsibility and find some things hard to accept."*

All the *Practice Nurses* thought there was need for more suitable resources. Three said that the main reason why they did not make use of health education resources was the lack of appropriate material.

Half the 18 *GP interviewees* said they made no use of health education resources. Of these, four said there was no need with elderly people: two thought their minority elderly patients could not read, and two thought they were not interested. Five GPs thought more leaflets would be useful, covering over-75s checks, use of primary health care services, diabetes, heart disease, strokes, diet. Most saw no use for videos. One saw a greater role for the Linkworker:

> *"You can't penetrate to (this group) so easily. It's difficult to get across that a health check is not to do with being ill. All we can do is send out letters, but if that's not enough we'd need to send someone to explain in person, e.g. Linkworker."*

The *Linkworkers* also thought that little was available for elderly people. Three thought that videos would be helpful, and one again emphasised the importance of personal contact:

> *"Some patients come from rural areas and don't have much education and can't read their own language so it's better to have videos rather than leaflets. With a video and face-to-face you're sure the information has been passed, not relying on someone reading and you get feedback straight away."*

Areas which they thought should be covered in additional material were diet, exercise, diabetes and information on services.

The range of conflicting views on the usefulness and appropriate form of health education materials in relation to elderly people from black and minority ethnic groups indicates a need for further investigation: the use of existing materials needs to be assessed, and further research carried out into patient and professional satisfaction and demand.

6.9 CARERS

6.9.1 Specific needs

All interviewees were asked whether they thought the carers of elderly people from any black or minority ethnic community had any specific needs.

Because of their role in the community, *Community Nurses* are well placed to identify and represent the needs of carers. Three of the nine thought that there were no specific needs because families coped so well. Two thought carers lacked information and advice on services, and two felt strongly that although families did cope in their own way with responsibility for the care of the elderly, they did not get any support. Some uncertainty about how best to help was expressed. The following quotes illustrate unresolved attitudes towards the needs of the carers:

> ". . . (family) care for the terminally ill is beautiful – we only have to give support; sometimes the daughter-in-law is quite resentful where her father-in-law is concerned, but not her own mother. (The question is) how to support? WE are important, we can give a lot of help, get aids etc. though often clients know what they want and where to go for it."
>
> ". . . (these groups of patients) don't have the same kind of social need – the demand for facilities for the (indigenous) elderly is far greater than the supply. . . . (Minority ethnic) elderly people are so much better integrated in their own family – they're not shelved – they still look after the children; they're seldom seen in phased (sic) or day care."
>
> "They don't have needs in the same way – the families do take turns. But there are family issues and sometimes you have to point out that it's someone else's turn because a daughter needs a break."
>
> "Respite care is needed because of family crises. This gives the carer a break but that's no different (from the indigenous population). But traditional cultures expect certain help from daughters, and the daughters accept it."

Other comments focussed on middle-aged women and those approaching old age, whose needs were rather different:

> "It's hard on the middle-aged group – trying to bridge the gap between the old and the young; arranged marriages are a conflict point."
>
> "The family situation is changing – young people don't want arranged marriages – in the future parents won't live with their sons. Some women, over 40 and older, are already very isolated and lonely. They live with their husband's family, while their own families have moved to a different town for work. (It leads) to psychological illness, manifesting as physical. The problems are not psychiatric – they are really loneliness and isolation."

Two of the *Practice Nurses* thought that the carers had no specific needs, and one combined an admission that she did not know much about needs with an assumption that things were satisfactory:

> "They don't make their needs known; they don't apply for things – just carry on, we don't really know much about it. With the families, they know that it's their duty and don't look for help."

The others all thought that carers from black or minority ethnic communities had the same needs as the indigenous population for information on the facilities available and support groups. Four of the Practice Nurses said that there were no specific services for carers in their area, but one said that the local Asian day centre had taken up the issue of carers' needs, and did a lot.

The *GP interviewees* were divided between those (nearly half) who thought there were no specific needs, and those who saw those needs as acute. A few said they did not know. It is difficult to explain the divergence of these views; they were not related to area. Like the nurses, some GPs saw the responsibility taken by families and saw no need for intervention:

> *"More families look after the elderly; they won't accept help because of cultural tradition. The daughter-in-law does the lot."*
> *"They don't use the facilities; they have a strong sense of duty and expectation."*

Some thought the needs were the same as those of the indigenous population, and some painted a vivid picture of the situation in their local area:

> *"There are pressures, e.g. accommodation. Care homes are not the answer. The family needs support – space, heating, an extra toilet – this is very important; it's a source of conflict, and anyway may be improperly sited upstairs."*
> *"There is no support – the family takes the burden, they could get some respite care if there were a day centre, not as a hospital, but if they could give medication it would be better. I have an 80 year old Asian female patient, and she is diabetic; she has about 20 family members, but they are all out at work during the day. There's too much stress in the community, and there's no outlet."*
> *"Many times I've seen a patient looked after by the family who assume responsibility, and don't claim the benefits they should."*

Seven of the 18 GPs offered practical suggestions of measures which would help carers. In addition to improvements to accommodation for extended families and the provision of appropriate day centres as mentioned above, these included appropriate paid carers, more special workers to contact and support the carers and inform them about what is available, self-help groups, a health visitor for the elderly, extra interpreters and respite care.

Linkworkers expressed a similar range of views to the other professional groups. Two of the seven felt that the carers' needs were the same as those of the carers in the indigenous population; two were unsure about the situation of carers; two felt that there were significant unmet needs:

> *"Carers don't even realise that there is a support network they could have – they feel alone with their burdens. They don't know they can get a break, there is a big gap here."*

"There's a myth the families automatically take care of the elderly – there should be Asian paid carers. These are the first generation to expect the nuclear family system. White people like to have their own house, and not have room for elderly relatives, but because they're dependent they don't want to say anything."

6.9.2 Specific local services for carers

All interviewees were asked whether there were any specific services or support groups for any of the carers of elderly people from black or minority ethnic groups in their area; and whether they thought the needs of carers in their area were adequately or appropriately met.

Four of the nine *Community Nurses* said that there were no specific services in their area. Most felt that needs were not adequately met, but saw it as a problematical issue:

"It's a 50/50 question. Do they want help? Are they able to persuade the client to let go of tradition and cultural background. As much as the carer might want, client doesn't want their carer replaced by foreigners."
"I don't think any carer is well supported; they could always do with more respite care, and day hospitals and nurses able to spend more time and not be rushing in and out hunted by time."
"No. Their needs in terms of respite and day care are not adequately met. The carers need a break, but the elderly people are reluctant to attend. It would be better if there were specific days or centres, with Linkworkers to help – that would be positive."

Practice Nurses' views on carers needs were polarised, with half believing that carers had no specific needs, and half certain that carers' needs were not adequately met in their area.

Four *GP interviewees* identified sources of support for carers in their area. These included Linkworkers, a day centre, a community centre and local Asian social workers. None of these resources was specifically dedicated to carers. Five thought needs were adequately met; two did not know; and the others could see a need for further support.

Linkworkers also had mixed views on the needs of carers, and expressed some uncertainty about them and the extent of their needs. One said there was nothing for carers in her area. One felt that the children were a resource because of their excellent command of the languages. Another said that the local Social Services Department was setting up a sitting service.

One of the Linkworkers worked in an area where a carers' support group funded by the King's Fund Centre was in the process of being set up, and thought that the carers were well supported, although in fact this project would directly benefit only one minority community. Another Linkworker had been involved in setting up a joint local research project looking into the numbers, location and needs of the ethnic minority elderly and their carers, a particularly exciting development since there had been very little service development for ethnic minority communities in this area.

In spite of the limited nature of the available support described, in answer to the question as to whether the carers' needs were adequately met in their area, two Linkworkers said that they were. Three said they did not know; one of these emphasised that this ignorance was because the carers had never been asked. Carers did, however, appear to need the services of the Linkworkers. In response to a question on whether the Linkworkers' services were needed by carers, while two Linkworkers said they had never interpreted for carers, two said they interpreted for them occasionally, especially where there were inter-generational differences, and one said that informally she often did.

Some of the comments quoted above indicate the complacency about family care amongst minority ethnic communities of which health professionals have been accused. The attitudes and perceptions of the various professional groups towards carers do not seem to differ markedly.

Other comments do not suggest so much a 'blindness' to need as uncertainty or passivity in the face of it. Some of this uncertainty is understandable. The tensions created by the processes of change and the pressures on traditional relationships within some communities living in this country cannot be easily tackled from within the communities themselves. They present a consider-able challenge to an outside professional group with limited human relations training, living in a society based on a nuclear family structure, and which is struggling to provide a decent and dignified level of care for its own elderly people.

Other interviewees did testify to needs among carers which though acute and widespread, are complex and require sensitive approaches with the full participation of the families and communities concerned. It does seem that a great deal more support could be given to the carers who choose to carry on taking the majority of the responsibility for their elderly relatives. This support needs to be tailored to the needs of individual families and requires a flexible approach. The needs of carers of elderly black and minority ethnic people is an issue which is just beginning to be addressed. The King's Fund Centre, in response to demands from community organisations working with carers, has funded both the provision of appropriate information on services, and minority carers' support groups.

6.10 ATTITUDES AND PERCEPTIONS

6.10.1 Reasons for high consultation rates

As in the GP postal survey, nurse and Linkworker interviewees were reminded that many surveys have shown GP consultation rates of elderly people from black and minority ethnic groups to be higher than those of the elderly indigenous population; and asked how they would account for this.

Responses followed the same pattern as those given in the GP postal survey. Two *Community Nurses* said this was not true in their experience. Only one mentioned higher health risks. One mentioned return visits due to poor communication and, in common with a minority of GPs, another mentioned the fact that the service was free.

The *Practice Nurses* had a similar range of views. One also mentioned isolation and loneliness, factors which the Linkworkers also highlighted, along with poorer health.

6.10.2 Views on whether primary health care is satisfactory

All interviewees were asked whether they thought the level of primary health care received by different groups of elderly people from black or minority ethnic groups in their area was appropriate or satisfactory.

Three of the nine *Community Nurses* felt that the level of care was good, qualified in one case by the view that the services were not well enough publicised to these patients. Others were equally certain that the services were not geting through to this patient group. One also identified a major gap in the provision of counselling and mental health services, and felt that nothing was available for these patients in bereavement counselling, alcohol or mental health problems.

A slightly higher proportion of the *Practice Nurses* felt that the level of primary health care received in their area was good. Two, however, thought that the low take-up of facilities was evidence that the services were simply not getting through.

Ten of the 18 *GP interviewees* thought the level of care was appropriate with a few riders about people not knowing the service was there, and not using it. Two were unsure. Five thought that the level of care was not satisfactory:

> *"It's highly unsatisfactory probably; elderly women are confined to the house cooking; the men are a bit more mobile."*
> *"No, there's a lack of care facilities, home care, community care, health visitors, social workers, community nurses and a Linkworker sadly lacking."*

"In some areas there are poor facilities, the minimum is done."

"I don't think we're missing any important conditions – little things which are important are quite often missed, particularly where mental health problems are concerned. I had one elderly Asian schizophrenic and the hospital had great difficulty, and they kept ringing me to go there. I said I'd love to, but I can't – sometimes it's my patient, sometimes patients of other doctors."

A similar division of views existed among the *Linkworkers*. Two thought that the level of care was good, "a lot better than they'd get at home", one said it was not and that the "GPs were not rooting for the elderly", and one was reluctant to speak for a community who had not been consulted.

These answers show that a substantial number of interviewees from all groups felt that elderly people from black or ethnic minorities in their area were not getting adequate services. Variation in opinion was not related to area.

6.10.3   Views on the contribution of service managers

All interviewees were reminded that the recent White Paper put considerable emphasis on quality of care. In what ways did they consider that service managers could ensure that all groups of elderly people from black or minority ethnic groups received appropriate and satisfactory primary health care services?

This was a question which at least one *Community Nurse* found overwhelming:

"There are so many areas to be addressed – I was thinking of upgrading the information on services to (all) elderly. It's surprising how many people are painfully unaware of what's available, and then if facilities are available, they haven't got the staff or resources to run as efficiently and effectively as you'd like; social services assess for handrail, then there's a six month waiting list . . . so services for minority ethnic elderly have to be thought of in this sort of context."

The need for better information about services was echoed by others, while three Community Nurses emphasised the more strategic approaches of quality assurance, needs assessment and service monitoring. However, one was unable to offer precise suggestions about how these aims should be tackled:

"Quality assurance has to be linked with packages of care being offered – people have to be aware of what quality is and buy the best there is. This is a new area and needs developing . . . there must be ways of monitoring and assessing. They have to have inbuilt measures of assessing."

The *Practice Nurses* seemed more detached from the wider issues of service planning and management, and one response was positively hostile:

> *"Get rid of some managers . . . there are too many managers, too busy getting rid of people at the bottom."*

The views of the *GP Interviewees* on the role of managers fell into three main categories which were (a) there's no need to change anything, (b) the efforts of managers only make our jobs harder, (c) some specific practical suggestions. The latter focussed on increased provision of appropriate community services, specific targeting of resources at the areas of need, training, coordination and liaison. One GP said he did not know:

> *"I don't know – does anyone know? It depends on us. Perhaps this is big-headed – all primary care for the elderly should come from the GP, whether for white or black."*

On the whole primary health carers did not evince great interest in strategic approaches to quality of care, and several did not see the work of local service managers as of immediate relevance to their own work. Although some had some practical suggestions, no coherent view of the role of local service managers emerged. The Community Nurses seemed the most in tune with current debates and developments.

6.11 DISCUSSION OF RACIAL OR CULTURAL ISSUES

6.11.1 With other service providers

As in the GP postal survey, interviewees were asked whether they ever discussed racial or cultural issues with other service providers who worked with elderly people from black or minority ethnic groups.

Almost all of the *Community Nurses* said they had. The main form which this took was participation in general cultural awareness training programmes, or multi-cultural/multi-disciplinary forums. Two had also been involved more specifically in reviews of the service needs of elderly people. One had not taken part in any such discussions, and felt that such exercises were not helpful:

> *"We do have a department for race relations . . . from what I've heard this can antagonise more people. I don't look for problems, just be aware of what could happen."*

Most of the *Practice Nurses* said they had been involved in such discussions. This was less likely to have taken place in general meetings than over specific issues which had arisen with individual patients.

Half the *GP interviewees* said they had discussed racial or cultural issues with other service providers, and half had not. These discussions had taken several different forms. The biggest single category was discussions with consultants about the needs of individual patients going into hospital. Other matters included general cultural awareness, case conferences with social workers, welfare rights, and women with gynaecological problems.

All the *Linkworkers* had been involved in discussing racial and cultural issues through local multi-professional forums, in training and cultural awareness exercises, through locality management, and with a wide range of local service providers.

The kinds of discussions in which the health professionals had been involved were general cultural awareness, or specific issues affecting particular patients. Most interviewees had taken part in such discussions. There was little participation in training forums on race in general, or on the more strategic service planning issues, although one interviewee reported that such discussions were beginning in her area and multi-disciplinary forums had been set up in another area.

6.11.2 With patients
Interviewees were also asked whether they ever discussed racial and cultural issues in relation to health and social services with elderly patients.

Three *Community Nurses* said they had not. Two said they discussed them where they felt it was important to ensure that the patient was aware of what might happen, or ought to be receiving benefits. Two emphasised the personal rewards of becoming closer to local communities:

> *"The women have their own network of friends – they're very*
> *supportive of each other, and they look on the nurses as wonderful.*
> *They're lovely, I'm always made so welcome and offered food and drink.*
> *I love the food – I eat it any time."*
> *"I often sit and talk."*

One of the *Practice Nurses* said the same,

> *"(I ask about) their ways of life through their relatives, and where*
> *they used to live. It's out of interest for me, not for health promotion."*

Generally, however, the Practice Nurses did not discuss racial or cultural issues with their patients.

In contrast, only three of the *GP interviewees* did not discuss such issues with patients. Topics covered general matters of culture, religion and diets, problems related to going into hospital, and family problems.

Rather unexpectedly, more than half the *Linkworkers* did not discuss such matters with patients. The two who said they did had very different interests. One encouraged them to assert their needs more, while the other was more interested in finding out about traditional health beliefs, and where patients "were coming from". Two had taken up individual cases with service providers.

It appears from these comments that while for some health professionals open acknowledgement of cultural or ethnic difference is an important part of their approach to patients, with many others it is not recognised, at least explicitly. This divergence cuts across professional groups.

6.12   OTHER AGENCIES

Nurses and Linkworkers were asked a question similar to that in the GP postal survey, but not about specific services for elderly people from black or minority ethnic groups: was there any agency or professional which they found particularly useful when dealing with such patients?

Community Nurse responses were quite different from those given in the GP postal survey. GPs had most frequently and rather vaguely mentioned social services. The Community Nurses were much more specific and without exception identified local specialist staff, mainly from minority ethnic backgrounds, who were employed to provide specific health services to the local minority ethnic communities. These included health liaison officers, Linkworkers, staff at the community centres, a specific Health Visitor for minority elderly, and the local Asian GPs.

Like the GP respondents, most of the *Practice Nurses* mentioned social services as the major source of help.

The *Linkworkers* mentioned a wider range of sources which included social services, racial equality units, Age Concern, and their colleagues generally. This breadth probably reflects the wide brief and community based nature of their work.

6.13   TRAINING AND EDUCATION

Nurse interviewees were asked whether they had ever had any education or training in racial or cultural issues; if they had, whether any of it related to elderly people; what topics would be most useful in any further training in this area, and how it might best be given.

Half the *Community Nurses* said they had received no training, and half said they had. None of this training had related specifically to elderly people. Like the GP respondents, the main topic preferred for any future training was understanding of different cultures, expectations and beliefs. One mentioned language skills. Five were quite specific that training should be given by those working specifically with local minority communities, or from the communities themselves, or with a practical working knowledge of the issues, rather than by an academic or professional trainer. In this too, the nurses' views diverged from those of the GP respondents.

None of the *Practice Nurses* had had any training in these issues.

6.14 SUMMARY

These interviews covered a wide range of topics, most of which confirmed the results of the postal survey, whilst providing much more detail of people's underlying views and reported practices. The findings are summarised fully in the final chapter, in conjunction with those of the other two parts of this study.

7 SUMMARY OF RESULTS AND CONCLUSIONS

7.1 THE SURVEY OF FAMILY HEALTH SERVICE AUTHORITIES

7.1.1 The sample

For this postal survey, 55 FHSAs were approached from those areas of England and Wales with relatively high proportions of middle-aged and elderly people from black and minority ethnic groups. A high response rate of 80% was achieved.

7.1.2 Service developments by FHSAs

No consensus on service development approaches in relation to elderly people from black and minority ethnic groups could be detected amongst FHSAs. A range of different methods was identified in this survey. These can be summarised as the 'ad hoc', 'strategic', 'specific' and 'needs assessment' approaches.

In some areas ad hoc measures had been taken where, for various reasons, a need had been perceived. A few FHSAs were adopting more strategic approaches, integrating the interests of black and ethnic minorities into planning and management structures. Some had identified significant specific local needs and targetted substantial resources towards them. The most unified response to emerge, however, was an increasing reliance on needs assessment exercises.

Although needs assessment assumed considerable importance in FHSA planning strategy, the disagreement revealed on its scope and definition showed how far FHSAs were from developing a coherent model. Moreover, it was far from clear how needs assessment would ensure responsive service delivery to black and minority ethnic communities or specific sub-groups within them, such as elderly people.

As a recent Government statement emphasised (1990):

> *"Health authorities . . . have to identify the view of users of services and . . . act as the patient's representative, championing those views, to ensure that servics are delivered in ways which are more responsive to patients' wishes."*

With their growing role in the management of primary health services, commissioning agencies will have a prime responsibility for the delivery of services which are responsive to patient needs and preferences.

An outstanding need is to develop a framework which guarantees a high quality of care for individual elderly black and minority ethnic elderly people, and acknowledges that that quality can only be achieved through responsiveness to the different groups within our society. Only two FHSAs mentioned any role for the broader mainstream quality of care strategies enshrined in the White Paper such as quality assurance programmes. Audit, which could potentially have a crucial role in defining appropriate procedures for the assessment, treatment, education and rehabilitation of elderly black and minority ethnic patients, was not mentioned at all.

Perhaps not surprisingly the contracting process received little mention in the responses to this survey. FHSAs have limited discretionary powers in negotiating GP contracts, although this is under review. In practice, however, many FHSAs are beginning to look at ways in which their powers can be used to influence service provision, and particularly to target resources at groups with specific needs such as black and minority ethnic groups. It is clear, however, that the contracting process is not yet generally perceived as the key to the provision of high quality services.

Contracts are likely to be given a higher profile in future, and to have a local element in them. The role of service specifications will become increasingly central to the delivery of appropriate services, particularly at the local level.

The evidence of this survey suggests that the interests of black and minority ethnic elderly people are still seen by FHSAs mainly as 'special' or 'different' and, in many cases, as 'still under review'. This may explain why the majority of FHSAs still had no clear picture of need or policy direction for this group. The delivery of high quality primary health care to black and minority ethnic elderly is not yet perceived as an integral part of quality assurance programmes. Of course it should be borne in mind that the role of FHSAs as commissioning agencies is still developing, and that they have a very wide remit; this study only examined their work in one area, and could make no comparisons with their role vis-à-vis other sections of the community.

The differences in views, policies and priorities, and the unevenness of response towards black and minority ethnic communities and their elderly, which this survey has revealed, indicate the need for more discussion and information exchange between Agencies. There is clearly a role for further training and education. The interest shown by FHSAs in this particular survey, and their willingness to co-operate with the project as a whole suggest that such initiatives would be generally welcomed.

7.2 THE POSTAL SURVEY OF GPS AND THE INTERVIEWS WITH MEMBERS OF PRIMARY HEALTH CARE TEAMS

7.2.1 Response rates

A satisfactory overall response rate of 59% was achieved in a postal survey of primary health care services for black and minority ethnic elderly people, carried out on a stratified random sample of general practitioners. Response rates varied by type of area from 55% in the London boroughs to 63% in the counties.

Forty in-depth interviews with a random sample of primary health care team members were also carried out.

7.2.2 Practice characteristics
Comparison of the characteristics of the practices in the three types of area from which the GP sample was drawn revealed significant inter-area differences. Practices in the London boroughs reported seeing the highest number and proportion of elderly black or minority ethnic patients and were:
- more likely to be single-handed
- less likely to have access to a practice manager
- less likely to have computerised age-sex registers
- less likely to be staffed by women doctors
- much more likely to be receiving deprivation allowances
- more likely to be staffed by doctors from black or minority ethnic backgrounds, predominantly Asian.

7.2.3 Recording ethnic origin
Only 14% of GP respondents overall routinely recorded the ethnic origin of their patients. Slightly more respondents in the London Boroughs routinely recorded; the practice of recording was not related to the ethnic origin of the respondent. The practice did not appear any more common among other members of primary health care teams than GPs. This means that primary health care teams may not be in a strong position to represent their patients at a strategic level in commissioning and resource allocation.

7.2.4 Communication
A high proportion (76%) of GP respondents reported holding consultations with elderly patients who did not speak English; 30% saw such patients weekly. Proportions were higher in the London boroughs than in the other two areas, and significantly higher for GPs of Asian origin than for white UK GPs.

This finding is consistent with findings from other studies on choice of GP, suggesting that elderly people from black or minority ethnic communities may overcome communication problems by registering with a GP whose linguistic and cultural background they broadly share. This limits their choice and may restrict their access to women doctors, practice nurses and other primary health care attached staff. On the other hand, there may be advantages, suggested by the finding that Asian GPs were much more likely than white UK respondents to discuss the specific needs of their elderly black or minority ethnic patients within their practice teams, and to make translated material available.

7.2.5 Help with interpreting

The main source of help with communication, for GPs and all the nurses, was the patient's family. This was true regardless of area or ethnic origin of respondent. In spite of the heavy reliance on families, considerable dissatisfaction with family members as interpreters was reported. Inaccurate translation and embarrassment were the main problems for both white UK and Asian GPs although overall Asian GPs recorded significantly less difficulty. The nurses reported similar problems. As with GPs, they resorted at times to using children as interpreters, mime and other non-verbal methods of communication.

Practice team members were also an important source of interpreting help. 47 respondents said that their receptionists helped, of whom 19 were said to have been recruited specifically for this purpose. Low levels of use of formal interpreting services of any kind were recorded.

It may be concluded that many of the methods used to overcome communication problems in primary health care involve a compromise in standards of privacy, confidentiality, accuracy and thoroughness for elderly people.

The main source of any professional interpreting help appeared to be the FHSA. This is encouraging, but many primary health care team members expressed the need for these services to be expanded.

7.2.6 Interpreting and linkworking services

Some mixed views on the use of formal interpreting or linkworking services emerged. Trust in the third party appeared central to successful use of an interpreting/linkworking service. Trust did not appear to be related directly to linguistic or medical/technical expertise; it may be conjectured that it develops over time through the professional relationship between doctor or nurse and linkworker.

There was a lack of clarity or consensus on the precise role and lines of accountability of linkworkers. This needs to be addressed. Linkworkers, by their own account, offered a broad service to their elderly patients which included help in communication, community representation and meeting some of the service gaps in the provision of appropriate health education, information, advice, counselling and support. The breadth and significance of their role was reflected in the wide range of attributes which other primary health care team members felt that a linkworker needed in addition to linguistic and technical skills.

The impression was conveyed of linkworkers as a highly accessible service within black and minority ethnic groups, working widely within the communities (though these findings need to be compared with further research on the effectiveness of specific initiatives in service access to this group of the population, and on their acceptability to patients).

7.2.7 Health education and promotion

Sixty per cent of GPs in the London boroughs said it would be helpful or very helpful to have extra nursing or other staff to provide information, education and health promotion to elderly black or minority ethnic patients. Many more Asian than white UK GPs overall (64% and 38% respectively) gave this answer.

Nurses felt that the needs of black and minority elderly people for health education and promotion were particularly difficult to meet.

Few health education materials were used by any members of primary health care teams with black and minority ethnic elderly patients. A need for more appropriate resources was expressed by some, particularly on diet, exercise, diabetes and health service information. However, views on the value of leaflets or videos to elderly people were mixed, and the importance of face to face reinforcement of information was stressed.

7.2.8 Access to female doctors by elderly female patients

Findings suggest that greater difficulties were faced by elderly women patients refusing examination by a male doctor in London boroughs than in the other two types of area. They were significantly less likely to be able to see a woman partner and somewhat more likely to be transferred to another practice, referred to a practice nurse or other services such as hospitals or clinics.

7.2.9 Assessment, examination and treatment

The majority of GPs reported no specific difficulties in assessment, examination or treatment of elderly people from black and minority ethnic groups. However, Asian GPs were much more likely than those of white UK origin to perceive no difficulties. Where difficulties were reported, they were not notably consistent; the most commonly reported problem was lack of compliance with treatment, mentioned by 13% of GP respondents.

By contrast with the postal survey, most of the GP and nurse interviewees reported specific difficulties in each category, though reluctance to be examined appeared, not surprisingly, less of a problem to nurses. Nearly all the nurses mentioned lack of compliance with treatment as a problem. More problems in mental health assessment were reported in the interviews than in the postal survey.

7.2.10 Health checks for over-75s

There was no consensus of attitude on whether over-75 health checks for elderly people from black or minority ethnic groups posed specific problems. A majority of GP respondents to the postal survey (59%) thought there was no specific problems in doing over-75s' health checks for any black or minority ethnic elderly patients. Slightly more white UK than Asian GPs mentioned difficulties (44% compared with 34%), and respondents in the counties were slightly more likely to perceive difficulties than those in the other two types of area. The most common problem mentioned (by 25%) was communication, followed by low uptake (19%) and difficulties in assessing mental health (16%).

Other members of the primary health care team expressed a conflicting range of views on uptake and outcome; however, few problems were reported by Practice Nurses in actually carrying out the checks. It is clearly an area which will need to be carefully monitored.

7.2.11 Specific health needs or problems

There was no general agreement among GP respondents to the postal survey that elderly black or minority ethnic patients had specific health needs. GPs in the London Boroughs, however, were more than twice as likely (37%) as those in the counties to perceive such needs as existing. Even within this group, however, there was no agreement on the definition of needs which were seen as ranging from specific health risks such as diabetes to loneliness, isolation and socio-economic deprivation.

Nurses and linkworkers reported few specific medical problems, but mentioned social and psychological needs.

7.2.12 Liaison with other service providers

In spite of the generally acknowledged importance of integrating services for specific groups, GP respondents reported very little liaison with other agencies over elderly patients from black or minority ethnic groups. Only a tiny proportion of GPs said they had received information, guidelines or training on from agencies such as the District Health Authority or Local Authority. Very few reported any discussions even over specific cases. However, a much larger proportion of GP interviewees reported having discussed racial or cultural issues with other service providers, and nearly all of them had discussed such issues with the patients themselves.

In contrast, linkworkers reported extensive liaison with a wide range of agencies, usually with themselves as givers of information or trainers. Community nurses had also had considerable contact with social services and other health services, mainly by participating in training or awareness programmes. Practice Nurses were more likely to have liaised over individual patients.

7.2.13 Use of other services

Few GP respondents in the postal survey reported finding any particular agency or professional useful when caring for elderly black or minority ethnic patients. A very small number mentioned social services. Linkworkers, on the other hand, reported obtaining a wide range of helpful services. Community nurses emphasised the particularly valuable role of linkworkers, health liaison officers and other staff working specifically with black and minority ethnic communities.

7.2.14 Referral to other services

The majority of GP respondents (95%) and other team members identified no differences in how they approached referral of elderly black or minority ethnic patients to health authority or social services.

7.2.15 Knowledge of specific services

While some GP respondents were well-informed about specific services relevant to elderly black or minority ethnic patients in their area, the evidence pointed decisively to signifiant mismatches between GPs' claims about provision and those of health authorities and social services.

7.2.16 Reasons for high GP consultation rates

No coherent set of explanations emerged for high GP consultation rates by elderly people from black and minority ethnic groups, although it was quite clear that GP respondents did not attribute them to health problems. One-quarter, the single biggest category, said this was not true in their experience; possibly levels of service uptake are not clearly perceived. One-fifth attributed it to different health beliefs and expectations, and one-sixth said it was due to return visits because of anxiety or misunderstandings. It would appear that there is a great need for more specific health education and information for GPs.

Other members of primary health care teams expressed a similar range of views.

7.2.17 Role of primary health carers

Attitudes towards better provision of services for elderly black or minority ethnic patients revealed a classic concern for improvement in doctor/patient relationships. The most frequently mentioned way in which GP respondents thought they could contribute was through improved doctor/patient relationships (37%). Almost one-third (32%), however, thought that more specific services or facilities should be provided. Asian GPs were significantly more likely to mention a need for specific facilities than those of white UK origin, and less likely to emphasise the need for changes in GP attitudes. Very few respondents mentioned the current policy emphases on strategic approaches such as needs assessment, audit and service monitoring.

In a slightly different but related question on the role of managers in improving services, Community Nurses showed greater awareness of and interest in current policy issues such as quality assurance and needs assessment. They also stressed a need for better information about services.

7.2.18 Reasons for low uptake of community health services
A difference between the attitudes of Asian and those of white UK GP respondents appeared in explaining the low uptake of community health and social services by elderly people from black and minority ethnic groups. Asian GPs were more likely to cite lack of patient knowledge of services, language barriers and poor service response, while white UK GPs gave significantly more emphasis to family support. The testimony of Asian GPs to the difficulties still faced by elderly members of their community in obtaining services is a disappointing result after a decade of research, debate and service development. It is a problem which needs to be particularly addressed.

7.2.19 Carers
The needs of carers of black and minority ethnic elderly people were explored in the interviews only. Some interviewees were sure that no specific needs existed, because of their confidence that families were coping with care. Many interviewees from each professional group, however, thought carers were under great strain and saw a lack of any practical support. Attitudes within families and communities, and the lack of appropriate local resources were seen as placing specific barriers to seeking help. Several interviewees expressed uncertainty about how to intervene appropriately. In some areas little guidance was available or sought.

7.2.20 Education and training
Very low levels of training on racial or cultural issues were reported by GP respondents, 82% of whom had had none. The single biggest source of any such education was post-vocational medical training. To the extent that local factors are important in considering the needs of black or minority ethnic populations, post-vocational training is an appropriate forum and the inclusion of such topics within local training is to be welcomed.

A strong preference for training on such issues to be delivered within postgraduate courses was expressed. It is important to note also, however, that multi-professional groups run in collaboration with other local agencies were also favoured by nearly 40% of GPs. In terms of topic, a clear preference for information on religious and cultural traditions emerged. The emphasis appeared to be on a knowledge- rather than skills-based approach to better care for this patient group. It does, however, reflect the priority attached by GP respondents to the improvement of individual doctor-patient relationships through better understanding.

Half the Community Nurses had received some relevant training, but none of the Practice Nurses had. Like the GPs they expressed a preference for training on cultural factors. Unlike the GPs, however, they were inclined to emphasise the need for training to be given within the community by those with practical and immediate experience of working with local black and minority ethnic populations.

7.3 DISCUSSION

7.3.1 Structural issues

In focussing on elderly people from black and minority ethnic group as one particularly vulnerable care group, this study provides a means of assessing primary care delivery in the inner cities, especially inner London. Results have clearly shown that the primary care facilities available to many of these groups are poor.

Government policy over the last few years has addressed the problem of inequalities in primary care through, for example, practice improvement schemes, wider employment of practice nurses, and the deprivation allowance scheme which specifically aims to target extra resources at areas of stress. The Fundholding Scheme provides a key opportunity for GPs as purchasers to target resources directly at local patient needs. While several health authorities have taken extensive steps to improve the levels of primary care in certain areas, the results of this study show that in relation to the small but significant care group of black and minority ethnic elderly people, much remains to be done.

Any impact of recent policies on the target areas has yet to be systematically assessed. Continuing imbalances in the quality of primary care, however, are being acknowledged in the strategic planning for the future of primary care of some of the Regional Health Authorities (for example, Bosanquet & Lemmey, 1992). Some are proposing new structures for the funding and delivery of primary health care in areas such as the inner cities, including an extension of salaried service, and more flexible types of primary care facilities. The results of this study indicate that one of the key ways of ensuring adequate levels of primary care for elderly people from black and minority ethnic groups is for commissioning strategy vigorously to address the general issues of care in the inner cities, and monitor its impact.

It is important to bear this context in mind when assessing service delivery and development at the level of the individual practice. Previous research has established the link between standards of practice organisation and facilities, and practice capacity to innovate (Bosanquet, 1989). Inner city practices with low levels of nursing staff and computerisation would not be expected to take a lead in developing innovative or specific services for patient groups with particular needs such as elderly people from black and minority ethnic groups.

7.3.2 Service development issues

As reported, perceptions of the needs of elderly people from black and minority ethnic communities were found to vary considerably between GP respondents of white UK and of Asian origin. The latter were much more aware of the barriers to seeking and accepting help which arise from ignorance of services, anxieties about misunderstanding, limited health education and the lack of appropriate services, particularly in community care. They were much less likely to regard these patients as different, or as a 'minority' in terms of their care needs.

These variations had little impact on service delivery to this group, either at 'population' or 'individual' levels of care. The only apparent difference was that practices with GPs respondents of Asian origin were much more likely to discuss the needs of their elderly black and minority ethnic patients than others.

Few primary carers were involved strategically in assessing need and commissioning for black and minority ethnic populations; few were involved operationally in tailoring individual services to any specific need, although on the whole primary carers were more interested in this area. This was reflected both in (a) their perceptions that one of their own key contributions to improved future care for this patient group lay in better understanding, and (b) the priority given to the skills and knowledge needed to improve understanding in their self-assessment of training need.

Results showed that GP information about any specific local services for elderly people from black or minority ethnic communities was often limited, incorrect or vague. These findings are consistent with other research showing that GPs are generally a poor source of service information to patients (Roberts et al, 1991). Since GP contact rates with black and minority elderly people are so high, however, it would be useful for local health, social service and other agencies to target local practices as a key information point for these communities.

No conclusions about levels of unmet need in primary care can be drawn from the results of this study. It did not aim to assess this. Moreover, the needs of individuals and of particular groups within black and minority ethnic communities vary enormously, resulting in different levels of need within different practices.

What can be concluded is that even where primary carers perceive the level of care provided directly or indirectly to these groups as unsatisfactory, they do not feel able to give their needs priority.

Where service development had occurred, it was clearly related to the size of the black and minority ethnic population. For example, there was generally more ethnic monitoring, more employment of specific staff, more use of formal interpreting services and employment of linkworkers in the areas with the highest numbers.

Apart from these developments, however, it seemed that a certain degree of inadequacy of service delivery was tolerated, particularly in areas with lower proportions of this patient population. This was particularly evident in relation to the over-75s' health checks, where respondents noted high levels of difficulty in proper assessment while reporting few specific staff or other measures to address them. The results indicate that it would be valuable to monitor over 75s' checks for this patient group.

Clearly it would not be cost-effective to provide specific services in certain areas with lower black and minority ethnic populations (although it should be remembered that this survey only included areas with sizeable populations). Various steps could be taken, however, to supplement the service currently available. The cost of linkworkers, interpreters, or specific practice nurses, health visitors or community psychiatric nurses and pharmacists could be shared by numbers of practices or employed within community services. Specific services for mental health assessment and treatment should be given particular consideration. GPFHs may feel increasingly able to target resources at need.

In addition to this, there could be more dissemination of appropriate documentation and audio-visual material to meet the specific needs of elderly people whose literacy skills in any language might be poor.

Evidence on the role of linkworkers and 'health liaison' staff suggested that patients do not just turn to them for help in communication, but for the further health education, information and even counselling which they find it difficult to get elsewhere. Such staff appeared to be particularly successful in 'outreach' methods of working, and in responding flexibly to the community.

The 'linkworker' approach to working with black and minority ethnic elderly people clearly has a lot of value, and on the evidence of this survey it would be useful to extend it. Many such staff, however, are not trained for all the roles they play, and there is a need both to address their training, and to harness their skills more closely with community and practice nursing staff who have the appropriate health expertise. In some schemes this works particularly well, for example in diabetic liaison nursing care.

7.3.3 Attitudes

The results also show that many health professionals are unaware of any specific needs which elderly people from black and minority ethnic communities might have. These include the need for specific support for carers, the barriers to high quality in consultation which arise from communication issues and lack of privacy, and the impact of poor understanding on both patient satisfaction with the consultation and compliance with treatment.

The study also gave evidence of the need to address the attitudes of health professionals more generally. Some health professionals still approach these patient groups in a stereotyped and racist way.

There was also some unawareness of the major health risks to and true health status of black and minority ethnic populations. Very few respondents mentioned these in any of the questions related to health need or reason for consultation. There was also very little mention of the particular need of certain groups for preventive care.

Several studies have accused health professionals of 'complacency' about the responsibility which many black and minority ethnic communities take for the care of their elderly people. Insofar as many GP respondents of white UK origin quoted levels of family support as the main reason for low levels of demand for community care services, the results confirm the 'complacency' hypothesis.

A slightly different picture, however, emerged from the interview material. Many interviewees expressed awareness of the need for family and carer support, but were uncertain about how to approach intervention in this area which they felt was sensitive both within individual families and within communities. Again, however, such attitudes did not seem to have prompted them to seek help or guidance in this.

Comments indicated three areas in which this issue could be taken forward – further training for health professionals, the development of specific services particularly in home care assistance and respite care, and community development particularly in relation to women's needs, led from within the communities themselves.

The high proportion of Asian doctors providing primary care to elderly people from the Asian community in this survey provided an opportunity to assess any effects of service provider and patient sharing the same ethnic background. In terms of general practitioner services, the results of this study confirm the value placed by patients on ease of communication, which other studies have shown. It is important to note, however, that the demand for linguistic and cultural compatibility can take precedence in choice of GP over other criteria such as gender or range of services offered. For some elderly women the result of this was that their GP could not offer comprehensive care, and they were referred on to other services for primary care in certain conditions.

The striking differences which emerged between the attitudes and perceptions of GP respondents of white UK and Asian origin demonstrated the significance of ethnicity of service provider for understanding patient behaviour and need. As noted earlier, however, there was little evidence that this led to more pro-active stances in service development for these patients. It may, however, have led to higher levels of satisfaction with individual consultations. Twice as many GP respondents in the London Boroughs (where the proportion of doctors of black or minority ethnic origin was highest), as in other areas, denied high consultation rates amongst these patient groups.

7.3.4 Professional issues

The extent to which it is reasonable to expect those practices which provide the greatest amount of care to the elderly black and minority ethnic population to be most pro-active in service development has been discussed above. There are also professional factors to be taken into account. The majority of primary care in the inner city is provided by GPs of black or minority ethnic origin themselves. Such GPs are taking responsibility for care in some of the most deprived and stressed areas. In spite of this, they do not always have the support of their profession. The professional isolation of many of these doctors including barriers to career development have been widely documented elsewhere (see, for example, Smith, 1990). These are issues for the profession to address as an integral part of improving the quality of care available to elderly people from black and minority ethnic groups.

7.4 RECOMMENDATIONS

It is hoped that the detail of specific topics in this report will be of use to those interested in particular aspects of primary care. The results indicate several broad areas for action to improve primary care for elderly people from black and minority ethnic communities. The recommendations set out below focus on these.

1   Commissioning agencies should ensure that local needs assessment is designed to gather information on any specific needs of black and minority ethnic groups. They should make full use of the information already available from other surveys of the particular needs of these groups. Local surveys may add little to existing knowledge and consequently not be cost-effective. Ways of giving some priority to such needs must be developed. Guidelines for ethnic monitoring are available (Horton, 1992).

2   GPs should be encouraged to record the ethnic origin of their patients and make efforts to standardise the collection of these data.

3   Commissioners should take a lead in encouraging the shared employment within primary care of specific community and practice nursing staff.

4   Commissioners should encourage the further employment of linkworkers and health liaison workers for primary health care, promoting joint working with primary health care teams and joint care teams wherever possible. They should promote or support the training of linkworkers, and ensure that health professionals are given guidance on working with such staff.

5   All strategic plans for the development of primary care should vigorously address issues concerning the inequalities of service delivery, and continue to monitor standards of care in the more stressed areas.

6   Post-graduate medical and community/practice nurse training schemes should develop further training in relation to the care of black and minority ethnic populations. Basic components of training should include cultural understanding, health risks, attitudes and perceptions.

7   The uptake, quality and outcome of over-75s' health checks for people from black and minority ethnic groups should be specifically monitored.

8   Primary health care teams should become more involved in local needs assessment and health strategy in relation to elderly people from black and minority ethnic communities.

9   Primary health care teams should develop protocols for the care of their elderly patients from black and minority ethnic communities to ensure that lower standards for this group are not tolerated.

10 Provision for mental health assessment and treatment within primary care should be urgently addressed.

11 Efforts should be made to ensure that initiatives in professional development within general practice reach as wide a range of the profession as possible.

12 Community health and social services staff should consult with local communities on family and carer support, and develop services accordingly, particularly in respite care and home care assistance.

8 REFERENCES

AFFOR (All Faiths for One Race) (1981) *Elderly of Minority Ethnic Groups*, AFFOR, Birmingham

Ahmad W (1989) Policies, pills and political will: a critique of policies to improve the health status of ethnic minorities, *Lancet*, 1, 8630, 148–150

Ahmad W, Baker M and Kernohan E (1991) General practitioners' perceptions of Asian and non-Asian patients, *Family Practice* 8, 52–6

Ahmad W, Kernohan E and Baker M (1989) Patients' choice of general practitioner: influence of patients' fluency in English and the ethnicity and sex of the doctor, *Journal of the Royal College of General Practitioners*, 39, 321, 153–55

Askham J, Henshaw L and Tarpey M (1995) *Social & Health Authority Services for Elderly People from Black & Minority Ethnic Communities*, Studies in Ageing, Age Concern Institute of Gerontology, King's College London, HMSO, London.

Badger F, Atkin K and Griffiths R (1989) Why don't general practitioners refer their disabled Asian patients to district nurses? *Health Trends* 21

Bahl V (1987) *Employment and Training of Linkworkers: Training Manual*, Report of Work in Pilot Districts, Department of Health

Balarajan R, Yuen P and Soni Raleigh V (1989) Ethnic differences in general practice consultations, *British Medical Journal*, 299, 6705, 958–60

Beevers D and Cruikshank J (1981) Age, sex, ethnic origin and hospital admission rate for heart attack and stroke, *Postgraduate Medical Journal*, 57

Bhopal R and Donaldson L (1988) Health education for ethnic minorities – current provision and future directions, *Health Education Journal* 47, 4, 137–40

Blakemore K (1982) Health and illness among the elderly of minority ethnic groups living in Birmingham: some new findings, *Health Trends* 14, 69–73

Boneham M (1989) Ageing and ethnicity in Britain: the case of elderly Sikh women in a Midlands town, *New Community* 15, 3, 447–459

Bosanquet N and Leese B (1989) *Family Doctors and Economic Incentives*, Aldershot, Dartmouth

Bosanquet N and Lemmey P (1992) North by north east, *Health Service Journal* 25th June

Butler J (1986) Primary care in the inner cities, *British Medical Journal* 293, 6561, 1519

Chiu S (1989) Chinese elderly people: no longer a treasure at home, *Social Work Today*, 15–17, 10th August

Commission for Racial Equality (1993) *Race Relations Code of Practice in Primary Health Care Services*, CRE, London

Conroy S and Mohammed S (1989) Rooting out NHS racisim, *Health Service Journal* 5th January

Department of Health (1987) *Asian Mother and Baby Campaign*, Report by Director

Department of Health (1990) *General Practice in the NHS: The 1990 Contract*, HMSO, London

Department of Health (1990) Press release 90/311, 22nd June

Department of Health and Social Services (1987) *Operational Requirements and Guidelines 1987/88*, HC (EP) 87 (3)

Derbyshire FHSA (1989) *Raising the Issues*, Derbyshire Family Health Service Authority

Donaldson L (1986) Health and social status of elderly Asians: a community survey, *British Medical Journal*, 293, 25th October

Ebden P, Carey O, Blatt A and Harrison B (1988) The bilingual consultation, *Lancet* 1, 347

Evers H, Badger F, Cameron E and Atkin K (1988) *Community Care Project Working Papers*, Department of Social Medicine, University of Birmingham

Farleigh A (1990) Invisible communities, *Community Care*, 22nd March

Fewster C (1989) Trying to speak in tongues, *Health Service Journal* 27th July

Firdous R (1989) Reproductive health of Asian women: a comparative study with hospital and community perspectives, *Public Health*, 108, 307–315

Foster M (1988) Health visitors' perspectives on working in a multiethnic society, *Health Visitor* 61, 9, 275–8

Gillam S, Jarman B, White P and Law R (1989) Ethnic differences in consultation rates in urban general practice, *British Medical Journal*, 299, 6705, 14th October

Haskey J (1990) The ethnic minority populations of Great Britain: estimates by ethnic group and country of birth, *Population Trends*, 60, 35–36.

Hoggart K and Green DR (eds) *London: A New Metropolitan Geography*, Arnold, London

Home Office (1989) *Race, Community Groups and Service Delivery*.

Horton C and Karmi G (1992) *Guidelines for the Implementation of Ethnic Monitoring in Health Services Provision*; Health and Ethnicity Programme, NE/NW Thames RHA, London

Johnson M, Cross M and Cardew S (1983) Inner-city residents, ethnic minorities and primary health care, *Postgraduate Medical Journal*, 59, 664–667

Jones E (1991) Race and ethnicity in London, in K Hoggart and DR Green, op cit

London Interpreting Project (1990) *Directory of Community Interpreting Services and Resources in the Greater London Area*, LIP, London

London Health Care Planning Consortium Study Group (1981) *Primary Health Care in Inner London*, LHCPC, London

McAvoy B (1988) Asian women: contraceptive services and cervical cytology, *Health Trends*, 20, 1988

McAvoy P (1988) Find the hidden carer: a GP view, *Carelink*, 5, Summer

McCormick A, Rosenbaum M and Fleming D (1990) Socio-economic characteristics of people who consult their general practitioner, *Population Trends* 59, Spring

Marmot M, Adelstein A and Bulusu L (1984) *Immigrant Mortality in England and Wales 1970–78*, OPCS Studies of Medicine and Population Subjects 47, HMSO, London

Mather H and Keen H (1985) The Southall diabetes survey, *British Medical Journal*, 291

Maughan B (1989) *Production of Leaflets for Ethnic Minorities*, Nottingham FPC Family Practitioner Services

NAHA (National Association of Health Authorities) (1988) *Action Not Words*, NAHA, London

Richter R, Daly S and Clarke J (1979) Overcoming language difficulties with migrant patients, *Medical Journal of Australia* 1, 275–6

Roberts S, Steele J and Moore N (1991) *Finding Out About Residential Care*, Information Policy Working Paper no. 3, Policy Studies Institute, London

Smith D (1980) *Overseas Doctors in the National Health Service*, PSI, London

Solihull FHSA (1989) *Assessing the Needs of Those 'On the Edge' of Society*, Solihull Family Health Service Authority

Van der Stuyft P, De Muynck A, Schillemans L and Timmerman C (1989) Migration, acculturation and utilization of primary health care, *Social Science and Medicine* 29, 1, 53–60

West Lambeth Health Authority (1989) *Towards Informed Action for Health*, Directorate of Public Health

Wright CM (1983) Language and communication problems in an Asian community, *Journal of the Royal College of General Practitioners*, 33, 101–4

9 APPENDICES

APPENDIX A QUESTIONS USED IN POSTAL SURVEY OF
FHSAs

Primary Health Care Services for Elderly People from Black and
Ethnic Minorities
Job title of person(s) completing questionnaire

Date   Name of FHSA

1.1 Do any of the following groups in your area have particular problems in
access to primary health care services?

Over 60/65s in certain parts of your area	YES/NO
The over-75s	YES/NO
Black and ethnic minority elderly	YES/NO
Elderly people in residential care	YES/NO
Other (please specify)	YES/NO

1.2 Has this FHSA prioritised any particular *elderly* groups in terms of
resource allocation, service review, etc? If YES, which groups? In what
way?

2   Please list the main black and ethnic minority communities in your area.

3.1 There is a range of ways in which authorities such as FHSAs can
approach services for black and ethnic minority groups. Some ways are
listed below. Please tick any adopted by this FHSA. (PLEASE ANSWER
WITH REFERENCE TO BLACK AND ETHNIC MINORITIES
ONLY.)

FHSA has sought advice/information from DHA
FHSA has sought advice/information from LA dept
FHSA maintains list of interpreting services
FHSA keeps record of languages spoken by GPs/practice staff
FHSA employs ethnic minority development officer
FHSA has/used to have working group on ethnic minorities
FHSA consumer survey identifying views of ethnic minority groups
FHSA review of services to black and ethnic minority groups
FHSA monitoring of service use by black and ethnic minorities
FHSA adoption of equal employment policy
FHSA has had leaflets/posters translated
FHSA has advised GPs on issues of black and ethnic minorities

---

NB: This section merely lists the questions used; for reasons of space it does not
reproduce the layout and design of the actual questionnaire.

FHSA has advised other practitioners on such issues
FHSA gives/has given training on equal opportunities
FHSA has funded GP training/education on equal opportunities

3.2 Has the FHSA taken any OTHER service development initiatives in relation to black and ethnic minorities? Please describe.

3.3 Were ANY of the initiatives detailed above in Qs 3.1 and 3.2 targeted specifically at the elderly? If YES, please give details.

4.1 Do any GPs in your FHSA area employ linkworkers? YES/NO/DK

4.2 Does the FHSA directly employ any linkworkers itself? YES/NO. If YES, please give details.

4.3 Does the FHSA have any information on the ethnic composition of the population it serves? YES/NO. If YES, please describe.

4.4 Does the FHSA have any means of collecting data on the ethnic origins of its patient population? YES/NO. If YES, please describe the means.

4.5 What are the most important ways in which FHSAs can contribute to the provision of appropriate primary health care services to black and ethnic minority elderly?

4.6 Does the FHSA have any plans for future service development to this group? Please describe.

APPENDIX B QUESTIONS USED IN POSTAL SURVEY OF GENERAL PRACTITIONERS

Primary Health Care for Elderly Black and Ethnic Minority* Patients: GP QRE

*This study focuses mainly on Afro-Caribbean/Asian communities, but we are also interested in GP experiences with other ethnic minority elders.

Ethnic Elderly Population

1   What is the approximate proportion of all patients aged 65 and over on your practice list? PLEASE TICK.
DK/10% or under/11–20%/21–30%/More than 30%

2   PLEASE TICK the ethnic groups from which most of your *elderly black and ethnic minority* patients come. Afro-Caribbean/African/Indian/ Pakistani/Bangladeshi/Chinese/Other (specify)

2a   What is the *largest* group of ethnic minority elderly?

2b   What is the approx. number of these on your list? DK/Number

3   Do you record the ethnic origin of the patients on your list? YES/NO/ SOMETIMES

4   Do you have any other information on the ethnic composition of your patient population? YES/NO

Communication

5   Looking back over the last year, how often do you have consultations with ELDERLY patients who do not speak English? DK/Not at all/Less than once per week/About once per week/A few times per week/Nearly every day or every day

6   Are there any groups of ethnic minority elders with whom you have particular difficulty in communication because of language problems? PLEASE TICK all those which apply. Afro-Caribbean/African/Indian/ Pakistani/Bangladeshi/Chinese/Other (specify)

6a   How do you usually deal with those communication problems?

6b   What problems arise when family or friends help with interpreting?

6c   If you make use of the services of *linkworkers, interpreters* or *advocates*, could you tell us who employs them?

NB: This section merely lists the questions used; for reasons of space it does not reproduce the layout and design of the actual questionnaire.

	Practice	DHA	FHSA	LA	VOL
Interpreters					
Linkworkers					
Advocates					

6d   What problems, if any, arise in the use of such services?

6e   If practice staff help with interpreting, can you give details of which staff by ticking the relevant boxes below? Practice Partner/Practice Manager/ Receptionist/Secretary or Clerk/Practice Nurse/Health Visitor/District Nurse/Other (specify)

7   What would happen in your practice if an elderly black or ethnic minority woman were reluctant to be examined by a male doctor?

8   Are there any other specific difficulties in assessment, examination or treatment of any black or ethnic minority elderly due to *cultural differences?*

8a   Assessment

8b   Examination

8c   Treatment

Practice Services

9   Are any *translated leaflets/posters* relevant to ELDERLY black or ethnic minority patients available within your practice? YES/NO

10   Does the practice employ/allocate any staff specifically to provide a service to any elderly people from black or ethnic minorities? TICK AS MANY AS APPLY. No/GP Partner/Receptionist/Practice Nurse/ District Nurse/Health Visitor/Other (specify)

11   What specific problems arise in providing or carrying out health checks amongst any groups of black or ethnic minority over-75s? TICK AS MANY AS APPLY. None/Publicising service/Communication during checks/Physical examinations/Assessment of hearing or sight/ Assessment of mental state/Assessment of social support/Low uptake/ Other (specify)

12   How helpful would you find *increased access to a linkworker or special nurse* to give health information/education/promotion to ethnic elders? PLEASE TICK. No need/Helpful/Very helpful

13   Do any group of your ELDERLY black or ethnic minority patients have *Specific health needs or problems?* YES/NO

13a If YES, please give details of ethnic groups and problems.

14   Many surveys have shown *GP consultation rates* of ethnic elders are higher than the elderly indigenous population. How would you account for this?

Other Services

15   Have you/your practice had any of the following *contacts with statutory or voluntary agencies* in relation to ethnic minority elders? TICK AS MANY AS APPLY.

Questions	DHA	Soc. Serv.	FHSA	Vol. eg CRE, CHC
Agency has given info. guidelines				
Agency has given training				
Racial/cultural issues raised in liaison over individual clients				
Other (specify)				

16   Possible services which *Health Authorities* might provide specifically for ethnic elders are listed below. PLEASE TICK any you know of in your area.

> Interpreters or linkworkers
> Ethnic minorities advisor or officer
> Translated documentation
> Specific community mental health service
> Specific acute mental health service
> Community nurses with a range of languages
> Specific health promotion programme
> Specific health screening/clinics
> Specific day care provision
> Specific rehabilitation services
> Women doctors on demand (outpatients/acute)
> Catering for dietary preferences (inpatients)
> Provision for personal needs (inpatients)
> Other (specify)

17   Do you approach *referral* of any ethnic elderly patients for *health authority services* differently from the indigenous elderly? YES/NO

17a If YES, give details of which patients, and any differences.

18 Possible *Social Services* which might be provided specifically for ethnic minority elders are listed below. Can you TICK any of those you know of in your area?

>Interpreters/translators
>Translated documentation
>Specific residential care
>Specific day care/lunch clubs
>Specific meals-on-wheels
>Specific home help
>Other (specify)

19 Do you approach *referral* of any elderly black and ethnic minority patients for *social services* differently from the indigenous elderly? YES/ NO

19a If YES, please describe which groups and any differences.

20 Which, if any, of the particular services or professionals specifically provided for elderly black and ethnic minority patients do you make most use of?

General

21 Have you ever discussed racial/cultural issues in the practice team? YES/ NO

22 Have you ever discussed issues related SPECIFICALLY to the ethnic minority elderly? YES/NO

23 What are the most important ways in which GPs can contribute to the provision of appropriate health care services for their elderly black and ethnic minority patients?

24 Research has consistently shown that uptake of community health and social care services by ethnic elders is low. Why do you think this is?

Education/Training

25 Have you ever had any education/training related to the particular needs of ethnic minority elderly? TICK AS MANY AS APPLY. None/ Undergraduate/Vocational/Post-vocational/Other (specify)

25a Which topics would be most useful in any further training in this area?

25b How could this training best be given? TICK AS MANY AS APPLY.

>Lectures at postgraduate centre/local hospital
>Resourced discussions within GP groups
>Short block GP courses
>Multi-professional groups with other agencies

On a practice team basis
Audio-visual packs
Documentary material
Other (specify)

Practice Details
Respondent

26a *Age*	26b *Sex*	26c *Ethnic Origin*
25–35	M	White
36–45		African
46–55	F	Afro-Caribbean
56–65		Indian
66 and over		Pakistani
		Bangladeshi
		Chinese
		Other (specify)

Practice

27d Total number of partners

27e	Health centre	YES/NO
27f	Computerised age-sex register	YES/NO
27g	Budget-holders	YES/NO

27h *Staff employed in the practice*	27i *Clinics*
Practice manager	Asthma
Practice nurse(s)	Diabetes
Receptionist(s)	Hypertension
Other secretarial/clerical	Well-women
Health visitor	Well-men
District nurse	
Other (specify)	

27j Do you receive Deprivation Payments? YES/NO

APPENDIX C QUESTIONS USED IN INTERVIEW STUDY OF PRIMARY HEALTH CARE WORKERS

As an example, questions for linkworkers/advocates/interpreters are used here

Primary Care Provision for Black and Ethnic Minority Elderly People *(Primary Health Care Workers)*

Name of Respondent   Area

Job Title   Employer

Interviewer   Date

Section 1

1 Could you please tell me a little bit about your role here, and the content of your work? (PROMPTS: referral source of patients seen – GP only, self-referral, other; patients seen in surgery; patients seen at home)

1a Can you give me a few details about how your work is organised? How many hours per week do you work in primary health care services?

1b How do patients or doctors contact you?

1c Who is your line manager?

1d Which staff can you provide help for? (which GPs, which other health authority staff)

1e Which ethnic groups do most of the ELDERLY black or ethnic minority patients you help come from? PLEASE TICK. Afro-Caribbean/African/Indian/Pakistani/Bangladeshi/Chinese/Other (specify)

1f Can you tell me roughly how many patients you help each week?

1g How many ELDERLY patients do you help each week?

1h Do you usually discuss matters related to the contact with the doctor (or other members of the primary health care team) with the patient outside the consultation? If so, what kinds of things do you discuss?

1i What usually happens when you get to the surgery? Do you wait with the patient until he/she is called to see the doctor, or does the doctor see the patient when you arrive?

NB: This section merely lists the question used; for reasons for space it does not reproduce the layout and design of the actual questionnaire.

1j Do you provide interpreting services with other members of the primary health care team?

Reception   YES/NO

Nurses   YES/NO (specify which nurses)

Other   Specify

1k Do you ever interpret at the surgery for contacts between the patient/ doctor and any hospitals, services (e.g. specialists/consultants/ community health services such as dieticians, dentists, etc., appointments, other)? Give details.

1i Are there any differences between your work with elderly patients and your work with other patients? (PROMPT: Are the demands of elderly patients different in any way?)

Section 2: Communication

2 Do you think that the presence of an interpreter, linkworker or advocate affects the consultation in any way? (INTERVIEWER NOTE: Make sure that the possible effect on both the doctor's approach AND the patient are explored.)

2a What are your main responsibilities/roles in relation to the patient? (PROMPT: Do you help the patient in other ways besides interpreting; for example, giving advice or information (which topics), giving support, speaking for or representing the patient's point of view?)

2b What are your main responsibilities/roles in relation to the doctor (or other health worker)?

2c People like linkworkers, interpreters or advocates can approach the problems of communication in a range of ways, including through their linguistic skills. Do you use other approaches, in addition to using your language skills? If so, what do you do?

2d Do any difficulties ever arise in your role as 'go-between'? (PROMPT: Are there any conflicts of role? How are these dealt with? Who do you go to for support?)

2e In your experience, do any specific aspects of the contact between patients and members of the primary health care team cause particular difficulty? (PROMPT: Assessment/taking medical histories, examinations, explaining treatments, patient compliance with treatments, giving/getting health education and advice.)

2f Could anything be done to help with these problems. If YES, what?

2g How would you describe your relationships with the medical and other staff with whom you work?

2h Are there any differences between working with different types of staff within the primary health care team?

2i To whom are you accountable in your work?

2j What criteria would you use to judge the quality of a good interpreter within the context of primary health care?

2k Do you think there is a need for MORE services like yours in this area? YES/NO

2l Why do you say this?

Section 3: Over-75s Health Checks

3 Are you ever asked to help with over-75s health checks?

3a Do you think any specific problems arise in providing or carrying out health checks amongst any groups of black or ethnic minority over-75s?

> None
> Publicising service
> Communication during checks
> Physical examinations
> Assessment of hearing/sight
> Assessment of mental state
> Assessment of social support
> Other (specify)

3b IF PROBLEMS MENTIONED, can you describe the kinds of difficulties which arise?

3d Many surveys have shown *GP consultation rates* of elderly people from black and ethnic minorities are higher than the elderly indigenous population. How would you account for this?

Section 4: Practice Services

4 Do you make use of any videos, translated leaflets, or posters relevant to ELDERLY black or ethnic minority patients? If YES, which?

4a Which do you find most useful?

4b Do you think it would be helpful to have more resources specifically produced for any of your black or ethnic minority elderly patients?

4c If so, what?

4d Do you think that the carers of any elderly people from local black or ethnic minority communities have any specific needs?

4e Are there any specific services or support groups for the carers of elderly people from black or ethnic minority groups in this area?

4f   Do any of the carers in this area need your kind of services themselves?

4g   Are you ever asked to help in a discussion specifically with the carer of an elderly person?

4h   Do you think that the needs of carers are adequately or appropriately met in this area?

Section 5: Types of Service Provision

5   Do any of the practices with which you work make specific provision in any way for any elderly people from black or ethnic minorities other than making use of your services?

5a   If YES, what? Is it successful?

5b   If NO, do you think anything specific is needed? PROMPT: What is needed, and why?

5c   Does your FHSA make specific provision in any way for any elderly people from black or ethnic minorities?

5d   If YES, what? Is it successful?

5e   If NO, do you think anything specific is needed? PROMPT: What is needed, and why?

5f   How do you think primary health care services can best be provided for elderly people from black or ethnic minorities? Should there be specific provision, or should there be no provision apart from the mainstream services?

Ask if respondent selects specific provision (if not, go to Q5m)

5g   If specific services are provided, should they be provided separately or should there be specific arrangements within mainstream services?

> GP services
> Practice nursing services
> Attached district nursing services
> Practice health promotion/prevention/screening clinics and services
> Other p.h.c. services

5h   Why do you think it would be best to have separate provision*/specific arrangements within mainstream provision? (*delete as appropriate)

5i   What kinds of specific/separate* arrangements within mainstream provision should be made for different groups of elderly people from black or ethnic minorities? (*delete as appropriate)

5j   How do you think that health services for different groups of elderly black or ethnic minority people are being approached in your area – i.e.

separate, specific arrangements within mainstream or no provision apart from mainstream services?

Ask all

5k Do you think that the level of primary health care received by different groups of elderly people from black or ethnic minorities in this area is appropriate or satisfactory?

5l If YES or NO, why do you say this?

5m The recent White Paper put considerable emphasis on quality of care. In what ways can service managers ensure that all groups of elderly people from black or ethnic minorities receive appropriate and satisfactory primary health care services? PROMPT: Can they ensure it?

Section 6: Other Services

6 Do you ever discuss issues related to race or ethnic background with the other service providers who work with elderly people from black or ethnic minorities? PROMPT: social services, other health professionals, voluntary agencies. If YES, who? Anyone else?

6a What kinds of things do you discuss?

6b Do you ever discuss racial and cultural issues in relation to health and social services with elderly patients? PROMPT: Do patients ever raise these kinds of issues with you? Are there problems related to these issues?

6c If YES, what kinds of things?

6d Have you ever taken up an issue of this kind with other services on behalf of an elderly patient?

6e Does your local *Health Authority* make any specific provision for any elderly people from black or ethnic minorities? Please tell us of any you know of in your area. DK/Available

> Interpreters/linkworkers
> Ethnic minorities advisor/officer
> Translated documentation
> Specific community mental health service
> Specific acute mental health service
> Community nurses with a range of languages
> Specific health promotion programme
> Specific health screening/clinics
> Specific day care provision
> Specific rehabilitation services
> Women doctors on demand (outpatients/acute)

Catering for dietary preferences (inpatient)
Provision for personal needs (inpatient)
Other (specify)

6f Do you think that the services offered to elderly black or ethnic minority people are appropriate or satisfactory?

6g Why do you say that?

6h How do you think health services should be provided? Should they be separate, should there be specific arrangements within mainstream services or should there be no provision part from the mainstream services?

6i And how do you think such services are being provided within this area?

6j Does your local *social service department* make any specific provision for elderly people from black or ethnic minorities? Please tell us of any you know of in your area. DK/Available

Interpreters/translators
Translated documentation
Residential care
Day care/lunch clubs
Meals-on-wheels
Home help
Other (specify)

6k Do you think that the social services offered to elderly black or ethnic minority people are appropriate and satisfactory?

6l Why do you say that?

6m How do you think social services such as day centres, home helps and so on should be provided? Should they be separate, should there be specific arrangements within mainstream services or should there be no provision apart from the mainstream services?

6n And how do you think such services are being provided in this area?

6o Is there any agency or professional which you find particularly useful when dealing with any elderly black and ethnic minority patients?

Section 7: Details of Age, Sex and Ethnic Origin

Printed in the United Kingdom for HMSO
Dd299979 2/95 C7 G559 10170